WHAT ARE WE WAITING FOR?

What Are We Waiting For?

Finding Our Way in a
World Ever Changing,
Ever Divided, Ever Seeking

Donal Murray

VERITAS

Published 2021 by
Veritas Publications
7–8 Lower Abbey Street
Dublin 1
Ireland
www.veritas.ie

ISBN 978 1 80097 019 9

10 9 8 7 6 5 4 3 2 1

A catalogue record for this book is available from the British Library.

Designed by Jeannie Swan, Veritas Publications
Printed in the Republic of Ireland by SPRINT-print Ltd, Dublin

Veritas books are printed on paper made from the wood pulp of
managed forests. For every tree felled, at least one tree is planted,
thereby renewing natural resources.

Extract from 'The Spell of the Yukon' by Robert W. Service (p. 33)
from *The Spell of the Yukon and Other Verses*, Barse & Hopkins, 1907,
courtesy of Anne Longépé, Robert W. Service's estate.

CONTENTS

FOREWORD

Since his first book, *Jesus is Lord*, published by Veritas almost fifty years ago, many generations of readers have enjoyed Bishop Donal Murray's writings. We've admired how he thinks things through, opens up windows of perspective, enabling us to see the bigger picture. In this book, *What Are We Waiting For?*, Bishop Donal gently guides us in an exploration of what deep down we yearn for. Yes, so much of life is spent in a scientific problem-solving mode but we also need to come at life in terms of mystery.

Revealing his own personal reflections and prayer at this point of life's journey, Bishop Donal urges us not to lose sight of life's ultimate goal. Quoting Cardinal Ratzinger, Bishop Donal describes how our conscience, like an original memory within us, points to our origin in God's plan such that when we encounter truth and beauty and goodness, we cry out: 'That's it! That is what my nature points to and seeks.'

The echo of our original memory 'awakens the mystery which is the source of the restlessness that can find rest only in the Creator.' The restlessness points us forward towards the wonder and amazement of the Resurrection that draws us beyond ourselves and our world towards the fulfilment of our dreams and hopes in *the* Mystery that is God.

With a hope-filled wisdom of heart, Bishop Donal speaks a fond word to us of his Christian belief regarding the next life: 'the most fundamental truth that will emerge from the recesses of our hearts is not our sins. It will be our wonder and amazement at the unlimited love of God ... We will recognise the unlimited love that leads us into the new creation.'

Bishop Donal, as you approach the fortieth anniversary of your ordination as bishop, we thank you for your wisdom generously shared over so many years.

✠ **Brendan Leahy, Bishop of Limerick**

INTRODUCTION

In what has been described as a 'prophecy', Cardinal Francis George of Chicago, envisaging a world becoming increasingly antagonistic to, or at least uncomprehending of, Christianity, concluded with a positive description of the role played by the Church throughout history in rebuilding crumbling civilisations – a role which it would continue to play in the future.[1] He wrote that that one of his successors would 'pick up the shards of a ruined society and slowly help rebuild civilization, as the Church has done so often in human history'.[2]

The task of rebuilding was central to the vocation of Cardinal George's patron saint, Francis of Assisi, who, in the small, ruined church of San Damiano, heard the voice of the Lord saying: 'Francis, repair my Church in ruins.' Pope Benedict XVI commented on the wide implications of that call:

> At that moment St Francis was called to repair a small church, but the ruinous state of the building was a symbol of the dramatic and disquieting situation of the Church herself. At that time the Church had a superficial faith which did not shape or transform life, a scarcely zealous clergy, and a chilling of love. It

> was an interior destruction of the Church which also brought a
> decomposition of unity ...[3]

The instruction was not simply that Francis and his followers should restore one small church which was in a state of disrepair. When they had restored that building, they realised that their task had just begun. God had a much bigger project for them – to renew and restore the Church in great need of reform and of a renewed spirit of evangelisation among the People of God, in Europe and in the world. The instruction to Francis was a call for a 'new evangelisation' of the Church in Europe and all around the world.

In our time, we face a similar danger of failing to realise the real essence, and the scale, of what we are called to do. It is all too easy to focus our attention on repairing or redesigning the structures of the Church as an institution, seeking greater efficiency, well ordered procedures, new ways of working, ranging from new arrangements for cooperation between parishes to enriching the work of institutions, from pastoral parish or diocesan councils to episcopal conferences, to the Roman Curia, not to speak of the running of schools, hospitals and other activities of Christian communities. All of these projects are important, but the fundamental challenge lies deeper. It calls us to foster a new spirit of evangelisation, a new sense of being a Church of missionary disciples.[4]

Six centuries prior to St Francis of Assisi's responding to a call to restore a church, and indeed a continent, in decline, St Columbanus and the Irish monks who were his followers had undertaken such a task and left an extraordinary legacy that is remembered and valued in many towns and cities in Europe. Farinella writes, 'Bobbio, Fiesole, Lucca, Taranto, [J]umièges, Auxerre, Laon, Luxeuil, Liège, Trier, Wurzburg, Regensburg, Rheinau, Reichenau, Salzburg, Vienna, St Gallen ... are all European towns founded by, or linked to, Irish monks.'[5] Thomas Cahill comments, 'Wherever they went they brought their love of learning and their skills in book-making. In the bays and valleys of their exile they established literacy and breathed new life into the exhausted literary culture of Europe. And that is how the Irish saved civilization.'[6]

The mission of those monks was a unique contribution made by Irish people to the history of Europe. Simply to admire and celebrate that contribution, while feeling no obligation to continue the task the monks began, would be a failure to grasp the magnitude of what they set out to do and what they achieved. It would fail to recognise that their task and their heritage is our task too. The accounts of their mission are more than a record of past events – they are a call to action.

Today Europe – and by no means least, Ireland – stands once again in need of cultural and religious renewal. We might ask ourselves the stark question, 'Why does it seem so hard, in our time, to envisage an Ireland which would even begin to be seen as an "Island of Saints and Scholars" and of missionaries?' If such a future seems implausible, that would mean that we are losing, or have already lost, sight of the spirit of those who preceded us and on whose shoulders we stand.

This challenge is what another Francis puts before every member of the Church today: all of us are called, like Columbanus and his companions, to be *missionary disciples.* Pope Francis has written:

> In virtue of their baptism, all the members of the People of God have become missionary disciples (cf. Mt 28:19). All the baptized, whatever their position in the Church or their level of instruction in the faith, are agents of evangelization, and it would be insufficient to envisage a plan of evangelization to be carried out by professionals while the rest of the faithful would simply be passive recipients. The new evangelization calls for personal involvement on the part of each of the baptized … indeed, anyone who has truly experienced God's saving love does not need much time or lengthy training to go out and proclaim that love. Every Christian is a missionary to the extent that he or she has encountered the love of God in Christ Jesus … we are always 'missionary disciples'.[7]

Many Irish missionaries, in Europe, Africa, Asia and Latin America, and the thousands of emigrants from Ireland, most of whom would probably never have described themselves as missionaries, brought their faith with them all over the world. This heritage challenges us to a 'personal involvement on the part of each of the baptized', taking up that task with faith and hope, and with enthusiasm. Columbanus and his monks looked on a Europe in danger of cultural collapse as the Europe of our time undoubtedly is, but they did not sit back and do nothing; nor did they think that they could leave the task to others. Still less did they reconcile themselves to an inevitable decline, or even a disappearance, of Christian faith in Europe. They heard a call to a demanding, whole-hearted commitment which would begin to rebuild the Church.

It is never enough to ask, 'Why don't priests or bishops or those in religious life do something?' Anyone who is tempted to ask that question should first ask themselves what they could and should be doing themselves. We are *all* missionary disciples.

For Francis of Assisi and his followers, what was at stake was not just the reconstruction and repair of houses or churches or institutions, nor even the restoration of a culture that had fallen into disrepair. When St Francis was told, 'Rebuild my house', that meant: 'Rebuild the house of God, bring new life and hope to the People of God, to the Church of Christ and to every person whose life we touch'. This task is one we all have to carry out. And this is done not only by heroic and demanding undertakings such as those carried out by Francis and his monks, but by everyone who has heard the Good News and who has grasped something of the joy and hope that it brings to them and that it offers to the whole of humanity. We are all sent to 'go and make disciples of all nations' (Mt 28:19).

We should recognise and celebrate the extraordinary role of Columbanus and of Irish monasticism in rebuilding a civilisation in decline, but, really to understand their mission it is essential that we recognise that this was not the core of what they set out to do. Neither is it the core of the renewal that is needed today. In his address at the Collège des Bernardins, once a Cistercian college of the ancient University of Paris, Pope Benedict XVI spoke of the role of monasticism in building and rebuilding European culture. But then he pointed out emphatically that the real driving force behind the work of monks like Columbanus was something much deeper than renewing a culture in decline, a deeper driving force which is crucial to the rebuilding that we are called to carry out today. Pope Benedict XVI put it unequivocally:

> First and foremost, it must be frankly admitted straight away that it was not their intention to create a culture nor even to preserve a culture from the past. Their motivation was much more basic. Their goal was: *quaerere Deum* [to search for God]. Amid the confusion of the times, in which nothing seemed permanent, they wanted to do the essential – to make an effort to find what was perennially valid and lasting, life itself. They were searching for God. They wanted to go from the inessential to the essential, to the only truly important and reliable thing there is.[8]

As he so often did, here Pope Benedict XVI here pointed to the central issue, to the core of the challenge that those monks faced and which we face in our time. This deeper issue should be the principal focus for Christians in today's social and cultural upheaval. We cannot enrich our culture – indeed no culture can be enriched – without a focus on the search for ultimate meaning – in other words the search for God. If we see signs of a crisis and disintegration, signs of a lack of depth in our culture, the path we need to follow is the one taken by those ancient monks: to seek the deepest roots and the ultimate meaning of our existence; to seek what is absolute and lasting, to search for God; *quaerere Deum*.

Cardinal Sarah has summed up the central importance of those ideas:

> At the root of all crises, anthropological, political, social, cultural,
> geopolitical, there is the forgetting of the primacy of God. As
> Pope Benedict XVI said during his meeting with the world of
> culture at the Collège des Bernardins on Sept. 12, 2008, the
> 'quaerere Deum' – 'searching for God,' the fact of being attentive
> to the essential reality of God is the central axis on which all
> civilization and culture is built. What founded the culture of
> Europe – the search for God and the willingness to let oneself
> be found by him, to listen to him – still remains today the
> foundation of every true culture and the indispensable condition
> for the survival of our humanity. For the refusal of God or a total
> indifference towards him is fatal for man.[9]

Rebuilding culture and seeking God are not two separate tasks. It
was because they were searching for God, who is the foundation and
meaning of human existence, that the monks could begin to rebuild a
civilisation. We are living at a moment of history when it is imperative
for us to learn the same lesson. We experience all sorts of moral, social,
political, and violent crises around us, including the devastation of a
pandemic, but we cannot hope to resolve these issues unless we engage
with the fundamental question of the meaning of human life, the
foundation of culture, the search for God. As St John Paul II pointed
out: 'At the heart of every culture lies the attitude [the human being]
takes to the greatest mystery: the mystery of God.'[10]

> We need people who have their gaze directed towards God, for
> it is there that they learn true humanity. We need people whose
> minds are illuminated by the light of God and whose hearts
> are opened by God, so that their minds can speak to the minds
> of others and their hearts can open the hearts of others. It is
> only through people touched by God that God can return to
> humankind.[11]

In the short chapters that follow, I want to explore some of the possibilities and challenges for us as we try to find our way in a world ever changing, ever divided, ever seeking what Pope Francis has called the hope that 'speaks to us of something deeply rooted in every human heart'.[12]

CHAPTER ONE

How Can We Know the Way?

What the legacy of St Columbanus and the monastic tradition in Europe (which still plays a role) show us is the centrality of the mystery of God and the meaning of human existence in the building of a strong and well-founded culture. In such a culture, minds and hearts can relate to one another *in and through the unlimited longing for God* which is the source of all our restlessness, the restlessness which will remain, as St Augustine said, until our hearts find rest in God.[1] In a weekly Audience, Pope Benedict XVI quoted Columbanus and commented on his influence in Europe:

'[God] has taught us the way with his Commandments.
The first of them tells us to love the Lord with all our heart,
because he loved us first, from the beginning of time, even
before we came into the light of this world'.[2] The Irish Saint
[Columbanus] truly incarnated these words in his own life
... [He] spent every ounce of his energy on nurturing the
Christian roots of Europe which was coming into existence.
With his spiritual energy, with his faith, with his love for God
and neighbour, he truly became one of the Fathers of Europe.

> He shows us even today the roots from which our Europe can be reborn.[3]

Pope Benedict XVI went on to point out that:

> The expression '*totius Europae* – all of Europe' with reference to the Church's presence on the Continent, is found for the first time in one of [the letters of Columbanus], written around the year 600, addressed to Pope Gregory the Great (cf. *Epistula* I,1).[4]

We need to explore the comment by Columbanus that 'God has taught us the way'. The Apostle Thomas, even though he had journeyed with Jesus during his earthly ministry, was confused about what 'the way' could mean. He asked: 'Lord, we do not know where you are going; how can we know the way?' (Jn 14:5). That question expresses a real difficulty. It is impossible to draw up a set of instructions, a detailed road map, or to have something like a sat-nav or GPS, which would point to each upcoming turn on the road of life: 'In 400 metres, turn left; then enter the roundabout and take the third exit'. If finding the way was that simple, life would bring no doubts, no surprises, no uncertainties, no unexpected challenges, no amazing joy. But Jesus did not give us a map to provide in advance for all of life's events and decisions. The future always remains uncertain and, in puzzling and unexpected situations, it may not always be clear which is the wisest path to follow.

The reply of Jesus to Thomas' question was, 'I am the way, and the truth, and the life; no one comes to the Father, but by me. If you had known me, you would have known my Father also; henceforth you know him and have seen him' (Jn 14:6, 7). Jesus often answered a question in a way that does not, at first sight, appear to respond to what the enquirer was looking for. Instead, he points to a more fundamental question, to a more profound and more challenging truth without which any response to the question would be inadequate.

He did something similar when replying to the lawyer in the Gospel of Luke, chapter 10, who asked Jesus, 'Who is my neighbour?' Perhaps, the lawyer was hoping to hear a detailed list of those who should be counted as neighbours and by implication, of those who need not be regarded as neighbours. Instead, Jesus pointed to what being a good neighbour means, giving the unexpected example of a Samaritan: 'For Jews do not associate with Samaritans' (cf. Jn 4:9). Unlike the priest and Levite who passed by on the other side of the road, the Samaritan cared for the unfortunate man who had been stripped and beaten and left half dead (Lk 10:30). This Good Samaritan bound up the victim's wounds and brought him to an inn to be cared for, promising to repay the innkeeper when he came back 'for whatever additional cost may be incurred' (Cf. Lk 10:35). So, Jesus did not respond to the lawyer's question by suggesting that some people were his neighbours and some were not. Instead, he asked who was a neighbour to the victim of this robbery, and concluded with the instruction: 'Go and do likewise' (Lk 10:37). The real question is not who is my neighbour – as if some people were and some were not. Everybody is my neighbour. The real question for each human being is 'how I can be a neighbour to those who need my help'.[5]

Whatever answer Thomas may have expected, the way is not a roadmap. Whatever the lawyer may have wanted to hear, the idea of a neighbour cannot be reduced to individuals whose names are to be found on some limited list. To respond to either of those questions as the questioner may have expected would not have led towards an understanding of the central issue. So, when asked about the way, Jesus does not predict what the immediate next step will be, or what the future may ask of us. He tells us that *he is* the way, the truth and the life. Being on the right road means travelling with him, trusting him, as the companion who leads us and accompanies us into what someone I knew, as his death was imminent, called 'the great adventure' of his passage into eternal life.

Jesus is the way to what Shakespeare called 'the undiscovered country from whose bourn no traveller returns'.[6] He is the way; he alone has returned to guide us home, to our Father's house. That was his prayer for us: 'Father, I desire that they also, whom thou hast given me, may be with me where I am, to behold thy glory which thou hast given me in thy love for me before the foundation of the world' (Jn 17:24). His response to Thomas is not a description of the details of the journey, with all its twists and turns and fears and hopes, joys and disasters. His response is, 'Come, follow me', 'come walk with me'. He does not say, 'I am the one who knows the way'. He says something much more significant: 'I am the way and the truth and the life.' He himself *is* the fullness of life towards which our journey leads us. He is not just the way; he is the destination. Knowing the way means knowing him.

The question posed by Thomas is truly profound. If we do not know where Jesus is going, how can we know the way? Following the way means going where Jesus is going, or, to put it more accurately, it means going to *where he has already gone, to where he awaits us, in glory at the right hand of his Father*. The liturgy provides a summary of this truth: 'He is the way that leads us to you, the truth that sets us free, the life that fills us with gladness.'[7]

To see Jesus is to have seen the Father. That is the fundamental truth about our journey. A roadmap purporting to describe every twist and turn of the journey would be entirely misleading. Presenting a detailed map of what our future holds would be to misunderstand and distort the nature and meaning of human life. Such a roadmap – if it could exist – would lead us astray. People reading such a map would take it as a guide that would enable them to plan, to arrange, to be in control, to be well prepared for the wonders and fears, the joys and sorrows and crises that life presents, and, to be able, by their own efforts, successfully to navigate their own way to the destination of life's journey.

But arrival at our destination, who is Christ in glory, cannot be the result of the skill, competence, vision and foresight with which we organise the journey of our own life; it is not an achievement based on our efforts and preconceptions; it is entirely God's gift. A prayer composed by St Thérèse beautifully expresses that truth:

> After earth's Exile, I hope to go and enjoy You in the Fatherland, but I do not want to lay up merits for heaven. I want to work for Your Love alone with the one purpose of pleasing You, consoling Your Sacred Heart, and saving souls who will love You eternally. In the evening of this life, I shall appear before You with empty hands, for I do not ask You, Lord, to count my works. All our justice is stained in Your eyes. I wish, then, to be clothed in Your own Justice and to receive from Your Love the eternal possession of Yourself. I want no other Throne, no other Crown but You, my Beloved! Time is nothing in Your eyes, and a single day is like a thousand years. You can, then, in one instant prepare me to appear before You. In order to live in one single act of perfect Love ...[8]

The destination of our journey is a reality that already exists. We pray in the Lord's prayer that God the Father's kingdom will come and God's will may be done. We conclude that prayer by affirming that what we have prayed for is already the case, and will always be so: 'For the kingdom, the power and the glory *are* yours, *now* and *forever*'. Jesus, our Way, already sits at the right hand of his Father in the glory that he, our destination, has shared from the beginning. The way is not simply a journey along unknown roads on which Jesus, our Way, leads us. He is himself the goal towards which our journey is directed. The *Catechism of the Catholic Church* says:

> The final doxology, 'For the kingdom, the power and the glory are yours, now and forever,' takes up again, by inclusion, the first three petitions to our Father: the glorification of his name, the coming of his reign, and the power of his saving will. But these prayers are now proclaimed as adoration and thanksgiving, as in

the liturgy of heaven. The ruler of this world has mendaciously attributed to himself the three titles of kingship, power, and glory. Christ, the Lord, restores them to his Father and our Father, until he hands over the kingdom to him when the mystery of salvation will be brought to its completion and God will be all in all.[9]

CHAPTER TWO

A Missionary Journey

Understanding something of the Way, who is Christ, hearing the Good News is, in itself, a sending out, a mission. It is no accident that the central act of the Church's life, the Eucharist, ends with an instruction that sums up what we must do about what we have just celebrated: 'Go and announce the Gospel of the Lord'. That is a task for every Christian. It is said of Bishop Joseph Shanahan, the great missionary of Southern Nigeria, that, when he was at home in Ireland, he would always begin his sermons and addresses with the words, 'My dear fellow missionaries'.[1] The people he was addressing had never 'gone on the missions' as Bishop Shanahan had; many had never lived in Africa, or in any foreign country.

The idea that we are all missionaries is not new. In 1946, Dom Jean-Baptiste Chautard, a Trappist monk, wrote an influential book called *The Soul of the Apostolate*. In it, he recounts a meeting of Pope St Pius X with some cardinals:

> The Pope asked them:
> 'What is the thing we most need, today, to save society?'
> 'Build Catholic schools,' said one.

'No'.
'More churches,' said another.
'Still no.'
'Speed up the recruiting of priests,' said a third.
'No, no,' said the Pope, '*the MOST necessary thing of all, at this time, is for every parish to possess a group of laypeople who will be at the same time, virtuous, enlightened, resolute and truly apostolic*'.[2]

Addressing a large crowd in Limerick, St John Paul II issued the same challenge:

> By the sacrament of Confirmation [lay people] are ... endowed by the Holy Spirit with special strength to be witnesses of Christ and sharers in his mission of salvation. Every lay Christian is therefore an extraordinary work of God's grace and is called to the heights of holiness. Sometimes, lay men and women do not seem to appreciate to the full the dignity and the vocation that is theirs as lay people. No, there is no such thing as an 'ordinary [layperson]', for all of you have been called to conversion through the death and Resurrection of Jesus Christ. As God's holy people you are called to fulfil your role in the evangelization of the world.[3]

This role is not some optional extra. It is not something to be done occasionally or half-heartedly. It is a response that follows from having been touched by the joy and powerful hope of the Gospel. Pope Francis said it clearly: '[A]nyone who has truly experienced God's saving love does not need much time or lengthy training to go out and proclaim that love ... So what are we waiting for?'[4]

That is the fundamental challenge for all those who have heard the Good News: we have to ask ourselves, 'Are we people who have "truly experienced God's saving love"?' The challenge is as great for us as it was for Columbanus. Europe faces a moral and religious challenge like the ones Columbanus and Francis of Assisi addressed with such vigour.

A crumbling San Damiano is all around us, *so what are we waiting for?*

The words of Jeremiah apply to all of us who have heard the word of God and apply to all our hesitations:

> Now the word of the LORD came to me saying,
> 'Before I formed you in the womb I knew you,
> and before you were born I consecrated you;
> I appointed you a prophet to the nations.'
> Then I said, 'Ah, Lord GOD! Behold, I do not know how to speak,
> for I am only a youth.'
> But the LORD said to me,
> 'Do not say, 'I am only a youth';
> for to all to whom I send you, you shall go,
> and whatever I command you, you shall speak.
> Be not afraid of them, for I am with you to deliver you, says the
> LORD. (Jer 1:5–8)

Pope Benedict XVI saw clearly that believing and acting necessarily go together:

> Christianity was not only 'good news' – the communication of
> a hitherto unknown content. In our language we would say: the
> Christian message was not only 'informative' but 'performative'.[5]

Faith is not simply a series of truths we are meant to believe; it is something that we are meant to do, and indeed to be. Again Pope Benedict XVI said:

> the Gospel is not merely a communication of things that can be
> known – it is one that makes things happen and is life-changing.
> The dark door of time, of the future, has been thrown open. The
> one who has hope lives differently; the one who hopes has been
> granted the gift of a new life.[6]

The first way we bring the Gospel to others is through the hope and love and care that our lives show to others. As Tertullian noted, that is how Christians are recognised: through the lives they lead – 'See how these Christians love one another.'

A faith that would see itself as something to be passively accepted would not be the faith that sent the first Christians to bring the Gospel to the world. To be a believer means being a missionary. When the Eucharist concludes with the words 'Go and proclaim the Gospel of the Lord', it is not just a nice way of rounding off the celebration. It reminds those who have understood what has just taken place of their obligation to *live* what they have celebrated. Pope Benedict XVI explained why this must be so:

> The love that we celebrate in the sacrament is not something we can keep to ourselves. By its nature it demands to be shared with everyone. What the world needs is God's love; it needs to encounter Christ and to believe in him. The Eucharist is thus the source and summit not only of the Church's life, but also of her mission: 'an authentically eucharistic Church is a missionary Church.' We too must be able to tell our brothers and sisters with conviction, 'That which we have seen and heard we proclaim also to you, so that you may have fellowship with us' (1 Jn 1:3). Truly, nothing is more beautiful than to know Christ and to make him known to others.[7]

It follows that anyone who has celebrated the Eucharist and understood what they were doing is by definition a bearer of the Good News – a missionary disciple. 'Go and announce the Gospel of the Lord' simply states what necessarily follows from understanding what celebrating the Eucharist means.

CHAPTER THREE

The Way of Wonder

The dedication, the enthusiasm, the self-sacrificing commitment of people like St Columbanus are still to be found in our time. We can think of many examples of dedicated witnesses to the Good News, not only in the saints but also in the humble heroism we witness around us. The first means of evangelisation is indeed the witness of an authentically Christian life, given over to God in a communion that nothing should destroy and at the same time given to one's neighbour with limitless zeal.

Pope Paul VI said:

> As we said recently to a group of lay people, 'Modern man listens more willingly to witnesses than to teachers, and if he does listen to teachers, it is because they are witnesses.' … It is therefore primarily by her conduct and by her life that the Church will evangelise the world, in other words, by her living witness of fidelity to the Lord Jesus – the witness of poverty and detachment, of freedom in the face of the powers of this world, in short, the witness of sanctity.[1]

The traditional hymn *Veni Sancte Spiritus* asks the Holy Spirit 'to come and fill the hearts of the faithful'. The commitment of the missionary disciple is not an imposed, burdensome duty. It follows from a recognition that what he or she is seeking to share with others is the gift of the Good News which 'fills our hearts'. This brings us to the important theme of wonder. In expressing how human hearts can be filled, St Gregory of Nazianzen writes of this gift:

> Recognise to whom you owe the fact that you exist, that you breathe, that you understand, that you are wise, and, above all that you know God and hope for the kingdom of heaven, and the vision of glory, now darkly as in a mirror but then with greater fullness and purity. You have been made a child of God, co-heir with Christ. Where did you get all this and from whom?
>
> Let me turn to what is of less importance: the visible world around us. What benefactor has enabled you to look out upon the beauty of the sky, the sun in its course, the circle of the moon, the countless number of stars with the harmony and order that are theirs, like the music of a harp? Who has blessed you with rain, with the art of husbandry, with different kinds of food, with the arts, with houses, with laws, with states, with a life of humanity and culture, with friendship and the easy familiarity of kinship?
>
> Who has given you dominion over the animals, those that are tame, and those that provide you with food? ...
>
> Is it not God who asks you now in your turn to show yourself generous above all other creatures and for the sake of all creatures.[2]

The deepest wonder of all was described by St John Paul II. It comes when we try to enter into the whole mystery of the Incarnation and

Redemption. This, he wrote, gives rise to adoration of God, but also to deep amazement at ourselves. He adds, 'In reality, the name for that deep amazement at [human] worth and dignity is the Gospel, that is to say: the Good News. It is also called Christianity.'[3]

In his Encyclical *Fides et Ratio*, St John Paul II again stressed the importance of that 'amazement at ourselves' which goes back to the search for wisdom in ancient Greece:

> The more human beings know reality and the world, the more they know themselves in their uniqueness, with the question of the meaning of things and of their very existence becoming ever more pressing. This is why all that is the object of our knowledge becomes a part of our life. The admonition *Know yourself* was carved on the temple portal at Delphi, as testimony to a basic truth to be adopted as a minimal norm by those who seek to set themselves apart from the rest of creation as 'human beings', that is as those who 'know themselves'.[4]

CHAPTER FOUR

The Memory of Our Origin

What is the ultimate source of our understanding of creation and of ourselves? In a talk to a group of Bishops in America, the then Cardinal Ratzinger spoke of something like an ancient, profound memory of our own coming into existence:

> This means that the first so-called ontological level of the phenomenon of conscience [the level of fundamental reality and truth] consists in the fact that something like an original memory of the good and true ... has been implanted in us, that there is an inner ontological tendency within [the human being], who is created in the likeness of God, toward the divine. From its origin, [our being] resonates with some things and clashes with others. This anamnesis [memory] of the origin, which results from the godlike constitution of our being is not a conceptually articulated knowing, a store of retrievable contents. It is so to speak an inner sense, a capacity to recall, so that the one whom it addresses, if he/she is not turned in on him/herself, hears its echo from within. [He or she] sees: 'That's it! That is what my nature points to and seeks.'[1]

Morality is not something imposed on us from outside, it is about what is deepest and truest within us. Cardinal Ratzinger went on to say:

> 'The love of God is not founded on a discipline imposed on us from outside, but is constitutively established in us as the capacity and necessity of our rational nature.' [Saint] Basil speaks in terms of 'the spark of divine love which has been hidden in us.' ... Basil knows that love consists in keeping the commandments. For this reason, the spark of love which has been put into us by the Creator, means this: 'We have received interiorly beforehand the capacity and disposition for observing all divine commandments ... These are not something imposed from without.' Referring everything back to its simple core, Augustine adds: 'We could never judge that one thing is better than another if a basic understanding of the good had not already been instilled in us.'[2]

There is an original memory deep within us. Indeed, it is the deepest thing within us. It will continue to be an integral part of who we are, a reflection of the moment when as tiny babies we began to realise that we are not alone and to recognise the rhythm of human speech and song and music which we could not yet produce; when we began to sense the divine invitation which resonates in us and which enables us to recognise what is good and what is not. That original memory is a memory of the individual creation of each human being by God. The *Catechism of the Catholic Church* says, 'The Church teaches that every spiritual soul is created immediately by God.'[3]

Wonder is possible because our nature points to and seeks an ultimate fulfilment which is beyond our ability to imagine, still less to create. It exceeds any of the much-sought riches that the world contains. Robert W. Service sums up that deeper quest for what is greater even than the gold of the Yukon:

> There's gold, and it's haunting and haunting;
> It's luring me on as of old;
> Yet it isn't the gold that I'm wanting
> So much as just finding the gold.
> It's the great, big, broad land 'way up yonder,
> It's the forests where silence has lease;
> It's the beauty that thrills me with wonder,
> It's the stillness that fills me with peace. [4]

We can glimpse the wonder of our origin in some events and experiences. For instance, on YouTube there are some short videos under headings such as 'baby hears mother for the first time'. They record the moment when, thanks to newly developed implants or hearing aids, a baby who was born deaf hears his or her mother's voice. The little baby shows shock, excitement, puzzlement, joy and amazement and seems to be overwhelmed by the experience. It is a moment which shows the power of technology and of human ingenuity to change the world for the better. For the baby and the mother, however, it is a different kind of development. It is the first step in opening up a new dimension, not only of the world but of themselves and of their relationship. It is a step that is filled with wonder; it echoes the wonder and amazement of our own original memory. That memory is part of a waiting that is far greater: 'For the creation waits with eager longing for the revealing of the sons of God' (Rm 8:19).

Saint John Paul II suggested that wonder and awe at ourselves and at God the Creator *is* Christianity, and it *is* the Gospel.[5] It follows that this should be central to evangelisation, to pastoral care and to liturgy and to the whole life of the Church in the midst of all the challenges of life today. It is the priority for all of us, priests, choirs, readers, Mass servers and entire congregations, to try to ensure that our Masses and other liturgies are what Vatican II said they are: gatherings in which we express wonder at God's greatness and gratitude for God's gift. Speaking about liturgy and particularly about the Eucharist, the Second Vatican Council said, 'The sacred liturgy is above all things the worship of the divine Majesty.'[6]

Therefore it is the task of each member of the congregation – not just the celebrant or readers or acolytes or musicians and singers – to do their utmost to ensure that the liturgy does indeed celebrate the divine majesty, and in some way awaken and deepen the wonder and amazement which *is* the Good News. It is interesting to note Pope Benedict XVI's remarks at the Aparecida Conference of Latin American Bishops. In describing the arrival of the Gospel in their lands he commented:

> [W]hat did the acceptance of the Christian faith mean for the nations of Latin America and the Caribbean? For them, it meant knowing and welcoming Christ, the unknown God whom their ancestors were seeking, without realizing it, in their rich religious traditions. Christ is the Saviour for whom they were silently longing. It also meant that they received, in the waters of Baptism, the divine life that made them children of God by adoption; moreover, they received the Holy Spirit who came to make their cultures fruitful, purifying them and developing the numerous seeds that the incarnate Word had planted in them.[7]

CHAPTER FIVE

It's Not About Statistics

In the 1950s and '60s all seemed to be well with the Catholic Church in Ireland. Irish missionaries were bringing the Gospel to all parts of the world; Mass attendance was high; seminaries and religious houses were full; some dioceses had to send newly ordained priests to minister for a time in Britain or further afield because the number of priests in Ireland was more than sufficient and was continuing to grow.

One might be tempted to wish that such a situation would exist again. But some reflection might lead to a different conclusion. During that age of apparently excellent statistics, the danger of taking pride in our 'success', of thinking ourselves as better than others, might be summed up in a phrase that one sometimes heard during those years: 'We must be the envy of the Catholic world!' That claim should have given us pause. It uncomfortably echoes the 'prayer' of the Pharisee: 'God, I thank Thee that I am not like other men' (cf. Lk 18:9–11).

The years that followed showed how mistaken that sense of complacency was, and Pope Benedict XVI's 2011 *Pastoral Letter to the Catholics of Ireland* began by saying that there was no room for complacency:

> I have been deeply disturbed by the information which has come
> to light regarding the abuse of children and vulnerable young
> people by members of the Church in Ireland, particularly by
> priests and religious. I can only share in the dismay and the sense
> of betrayal that so many of you have experienced on learning of
> these sinful and criminal acts and the way Church authorities in
> Ireland dealt with them.[1]

The goal of sharing the Good News with the world has never been about satisfactory statistics; nor about telling ourselves that we are 'doing a great job!' Above all, it is not about imagining that we are superior to other people. Being a genuine missionary disciple would never allow us to sit back and relax, satisfied with ourselves. Missionary discipleship is about the permanent sense of urgency which fills anyone who has begun to experience wonder and amazement at God, at all creation, and at what the Gospel offers to humanity. Once again, it was Pope Benedict XVI who summed this up by pointing out how the obligation to share the Gospel appeared to the early Church:

> Christians of the nascent Church did not regard their missionary
> proclamation as propaganda, designed to enlarge their particular
> group, but as an inner necessity, consequent upon the nature
> of their faith: the God in whom they believed was the God of
> all people, the one, true God, who had revealed himself in the
> history of Israel and ultimately in his Son, thereby supplying
> the answer which was of concern to everyone and for which all
> people, in their innermost hearts, are waiting. The universality
> of God, and of reason open towards him, is what gave them the
> motivation – indeed, the obligation – to proclaim the message.[2]

Spreading the Good News of God's invitation to humanity can indeed bring salvation to great numbers. When it does, that is not our achievement; it is God's gift, a gift offered to all not by us but by God. The missionary disciple does not give to others something that is his or her own to give. Gabriel Marcel says:

> All that we can propose to ourselves is in the last analysis, to waken within the other the consciousness of what he [or she] is, or more precisely of [their] divine filiation, to teach [them] to see [themselves] as the children of God through the love that is shown them.[3]

The missionary disciple's role is to reawaken what Cardinal Ratzinger called 'the memory of our origin'. That memory is also a glimpse of what God has prepared for his people (cf. 1 Cor 2:9). The Book of Revelation (7:9–12) says:

> After this I looked, and behold, a great multitude which no man could number, from every nation, from all tribes and peoples and tongues, standing before the throne and before the Lamb, clothed in white robes, with palm branches in their hands, and crying out with a loud voice, 'Salvation belongs to our God who sits upon the throne, and to the Lamb!' And all the angels stood round the throne and round the elders and the four living creatures, and they fell on their faces before the throne and worshiped God, saying, 'Amen! Blessing and glory and wisdom and thanksgiving and honour and power and might be to our God for ever and ever! Amen.'

CHAPTER SIX

Let Us Not Seek en Route What We Shall Be in Our Homeland

In his book on Columbanus, the late Cardinal Ó Fiaich wrote:

> St Columbanus knew the importance of recognising that being on the road of life, pleasant, joyful and full of wonder as that may sometimes be, falls infinitely short of what awaits us at our destination. To travel the road as if we had already arrived would be to miss the meaning of our journey. If we settle for what surrounds us on the familiar road of life, we may lose sight of the vision of our homeland. Saint Columbanus summed this up: Let us not seek *en route* what we shall be in our homeland. Some are really so careless on this journey, that they seem to be not so much en route as at home. Here on the road.[1]

This points to a critical issue for making the Gospel heard in the world of today. What would it mean to make oneself at home in the journey rather than in the destination? The road of our life is no doubt full of wonder and beauty, but it will not satisfy all the longing of the human heart. Seeing this life as our final destination would mean settling down to what we have, feeling that the life we experience from day to day is enough, or at least the best we can hope for, and to seeking no further goal than what the road has to offer. Our life along the road may pose many problems, some of which we can at least occasionally resolve, but we may fail to see life as what it really is – a mystery that cannot be solved by our own ingenuity. Gabriel Marcel sums up the difference:

> A problem is something which I meet, which I find complete before me, but which I can therefore lay siege to and reduce. But a mystery is something in which I myself am involved, and it can therefore only be thought of as a 'sphere where the distinction between what is in me and what is before me loses its meaning and its initial validity'. A genuine problem is subject to an appropriate technique by the exercise of which it is defined; whereas a mystery, by definition, defies every conceivable technique. It is, no doubt, always possible (logically and psychologically) to degrade a mystery so as to turn it into a problem. But this is a fundamentally vicious proceeding, whose springs might perhaps be discovered in a kind of corruption of the intellect.[2]

Scientific examination and research lays out a problem before us. A mystery is something which involves ourselves and cannot be examined as if we ourselves were not intimately part of it.

Problem-solving is the field of science and technology, but coming to understand the mystery of ourselves is the field of philosophy, art and faith; reflection, worship and contemplation. It leads us to the ultimate meaning which every culture seeks. Solving problems and reflecting on mystery are two ways of approaching reality. Each has its own validity and each can be of enormous value. Since they seek to deal with what is ultimately the same reality, they will not, if thoroughly followed through, contradict one another. Nevertheless, each is asking a different kind of question about the world. The danger, to which St John Paul II pointed, is that the scientific, technological approach, which has achieved so much, might swamp the sphere of mystery and faith in what he called 'scientism':

> Regrettably, it must be noted, scientism consigns all that has to do with the question of the meaning of life to the realm of the irrational or imaginary. No less disappointing is the way in which it approaches the other great problems of philosophy which, if they are not ignored, are subjected to analyses based on superficial analogies, lacking all rational foundation. This leads to the impoverishment of human thought, which no longer addresses the ultimate problems which the human being ... has pondered constantly from the beginning of time. And since it leaves no space for the critique offered by ethical judgement, the scientistic mentality has succeeded in leading many to think that if something is technically possible it is therefore morally admissible.[3]

It would also impoverish human thought if one were to regard science and the exploration of mystery as mutually exclusive.[4] The fact is that they have been more in harmony than many realise and the role of people inspired by faith in the advancement of scientific knowledge has been very significant.

Though tensions have existed in the Church between faith and science over the centuries, people of faith have made significant contributions in science. Archbishop Joseph Kurtz has provided this small sample of Catholic scientists that tells a compelling story about the scientific contributions of people of faith:

> Augustinian priest Gregor Mendel founded modern genetics ...
>
> Cleric Nicolaus Copernicus first developed scientifically the view that the earth rotated around the sun.
>
> Maria Gaetana Agnesi, mathematician, philosopher and

> theologian, wrote the first textbook discussing both differential and integral calculus. She also sought to reconcile aspects of modern philosophy and science with traditional morality and theology.
>
> Georges Lemaitre, a Belgian physicist and Catholic priest, is credited with what became known as the 'Big Bang' theory.[5]

The great loss involved in following an exclusively scientistic approach is that it can consider only the road and not the homeland, which is where the road leads. It has no way of addressing the ultimate questions of meaning that human beings have contemplated since the beginning, since these belong to the sphere of mystery rather than of problem. In other words, they are about the meaning of ourselves and of our lives; they are about the truth, which is already within us, the truth which cannot be treated simply as a problem to be analysed in a detached way. It is a truth which infinitely exceeds our scientific analysis.

CHAPTER SEVEN

The Most Amazing Thing

I recall hearing the story of a missionary somewhere in Asia who was approached by a person who was fully involved with his own religious traditions but who expressed an interest in finding out what inspired Christians to devote themselves unselfishly to building and running hospitals and schools for the benefit of people they had only recently come to know. The missionary gave the enquirer a copy of one of the Gospels and suggested that he read it. Some days later the enquirer came running back, saying excitedly: 'It says here that Jesus rose from the dead! This is the most amazing thing in the history of the world! Why did you not tell us?'

If we do not find it easy to tell people about 'the most amazing thing' it may be because it can most effectively be spoken of in the language of mystery and meaning and faith, rather than in the language of science and technology. Here lies a fundamental challenge to sharing the Good News of Christian faith today. The Good News is indeed amazing, full of wonder. The effort to express that belief in scientific, mathematical, everyday words cannot rise to the significance of the 'most amazing thing'. And yet those words, or, more correctly, that Word of God, has already been spoken to us in person and 'has dwelt amongst us'. Pope Benedict XVI spoke of this in his address at the Collège des Bernardins, in Paris in 2008:

> The fundamental structure of Christian proclamation 'outwards' – towards searching and questioning mankind – is seen in Saint Paul's address at the Areopagus. Paul is reproached for: 'he seems to be a preacher of foreign divinities' (Acts 17:18). To this, Paul responds: I have found an altar of yours with this inscription: 'to an unknown god'. What therefore you worship as unknown, this I proclaim to you (17:23). Paul is not proclaiming unknown gods. He is proclaiming him whom [humans] do not know and yet do know – the unknown-known; the one they are seeking, whom ultimately they know already, and who yet remains the unknown and unrecognizable. The deepest layer of human thinking and feeling somehow knows that he must exist, that at the beginning of all things, there must be not irrationality, but creative Reason – not blind chance, but freedom.[1]

The crucial problem about all of this is that if reflection on ourselves and on mystery gets lost, that would distort even the 'human sciences' such as history, psychology, sociology and philosophy, by leading them to try to present themselves as scientific enquiries, like mathematics and physics:

> If science as a whole is this and this alone, then it is [the human being] who ends up being reduced, for the specifically human questions about our origin and destiny, the questions raised by religion and ethics, then have no place within the purview of collective reason as defined by 'science', so understood, and must thus be relegated to the realm of the subjective. The subject then decides, on the basis of his experiences, what he considers tenable in matters of religion, and the subjective 'conscience' becomes the sole arbiter of what is ethical. In this way, though, ethics and

religion lose their power to create a community and become a completely personal matter. This is a dangerous state of affairs for humanity, as we see from the disturbing pathologies of religion and reason which necessarily erupt when reason is so reduced that questions of religion and ethics no longer concern it.[2]

The human being 'ends up being reduced' because there are two essential ways of seeking the truth: on the one hand, the scientific, mathematical sciences like biology or astronomy which seek to solve and understand problems and phenomena; on the other, the way of poetic, contemplative, imaginative, empathetic, altruistic, religious reflection on the meaning, source and foundation of every human being's inalienable dignity. It would be a great diminishment of all humanity if these two paths to the truth were regarded as contradicting one another, as mutually exclusive. It would be a diminishment because the human community would no longer be built on a recognition of the meaning, destiny and wonder of human life. It would mean that the fundamental human questions about the meaning of ourselves and our lives, what St John Paul II called, 'the fundamental questions which pervade human life', would be seen as less real than the questions of physics, chemistry and mathematics. Yet the fundamental questions remain always part of the human search for meaning. Saint John Paul II listed some of those and stressed that they are part of all human searching and of many different cultures:

> Who am I? Where have I come from and where am I going? Why is there evil? What is there after this life? These are the questions which we find in the sacred writings of Israel, as also in the Veda and the Avesta; we find them in the writings of Confucius and Lao-Tze, and in the preaching of Tirthankara and Buddha; they appear in the poetry of Homer and in the tragedies of Euripides and Sophocles, as they do in the philosophical writings of Plato and Aristotle. They are questions which have their common

source in the quest for meaning which has always compelled the human heart.[3]

This may be seen as an aspect of the warning St Columbanus gave about the harm that we do to ourselves if we focus only on the road we travel, rather than on the homeland towards which we travel. The extraordinary achievements of science have created the temptation to conclude that only what is scientifically proven can be regarded as really true. Yielding to that temptation would mean undervaluing, or even dismissing, the great heritage of human reflection referred to in those words of Saint John Paul II. The quest for truth, which is a fundamental urge of the human being, has to be alert to the danger of looking at only some parts of the story. To seek to analyse and solve problems while not recognising the mystery which is also essential to our understanding of ourselves and of the world we inhabit would be to pick and choose only some aspects of the truth, while missing other dimensions.

CHAPTER EIGHT

Both/And

We have seen several examples of what might be called dual approaches to understanding reality. For instance, one can approach the world as if it were a problem to be analysed and measured, as something quite separate from ourselves. We can approach reality as if the only effective way of understanding the world was through the scientific method, what Pope Benedict XVI and others have called – 'scientism'. But scientism risks relegating the question of the meaning of life to the realm of the irrational. Alternatively, as we've said previously, one might see reality as a mystery of which we are an integral part, a mystery which points to the ultimate questions about the meaning of our lives.

Patricia Kieran, of Mary Immaculate College in Limerick, points to the importance of an approach which recognises that science and other dimensions such as faith, wonder and imagination are not opposed to one another. She refers to Ken Robinson's book, *Out of Our Minds: Learning to Be Creative,* and says:

> ... his thesis is that schools kill creativity by operating from a partial and incomplete understanding of the nature and function of human creative intelligence and education. He argues that formal educational systems are heavily influenced by Enlightenment thinking and tend to promote a restricted view of knowledge and intelligence that is dominated by inductive reasoning. Formal academic environments tend to drive a wedge between science and the arts. While the sciences are viewed as leading to employment, the arts are devalued and seen as being more relevant to what one does in one's leisure time.[1]

The then Cardinal Ratzinger pointed to the need for both approaches: a purely scientific approach bears within itself a question which points beyond itself and beyond the possibilities of its methodology. Modern scientific reason quite simply has to accept the rational structure of matter and the correspondence between our spirit and the prevailing rational structures of nature as a given, on which its methodology has to be based. 'Yet the question why this has to be so is a real question, and one which has to be remanded by the natural sciences to other modes and planes of thought – to philosophy and theology.'[2]

A purely scientific, problem-solving approach would diminish our understanding of the wider dimensions of existence. It would never find the truth that can fully set us free. On the other hand, an approach which ignored the growth in scientific knowledge would close off a rich source for the understanding of our life and our world. We are faced here, not with an 'either/or' but with a 'both/and'.

Science itself points to the conclusion that a single approach to the search for truth is insufficient. But consider, for instance, the significance of the differing, yet mutually necessary functions of the two hemispheres of the human brain. They interact but they function differently. Since stroke damage to the left side of the brain leads to loss of speech, it was thought that the left hemisphere was concerned with language. This 'led to the left hemisphere being referred to as "dominant" since it did all the talking'.[3] However, it is not as simple as that.

The left hemisphere is not simply used for human language. The two hemispheres of the brain exist also in birds and animals which have no human language so there must be more to the left hemisphere/right hemisphere division than 'doing all the talking'. For instance, the left hemisphere controls the right side of the body as the right hemisphere controls the left. It also appears that the left hemisphere is more at home with logic, analysis and objectivity; while the right is more intuitive, creative, emotional and subjective. The two hemispheres interact and cooperate in various ways but they are not two separate brains:

> [The brain] is in fact a single integrated, highly dynamic system. Events anywhere in the brain are connected to and potentially have consequences for, other regions which may respond to, propagate, enhance or develop that initial event, or alternatively redress it in some way, inhibit it or try to re-establish equilibrium.[4]

A balanced reflection on fundamental questions often, or perhaps always, necessitates looking at them from a number of different perspectives, as, indeed, our brain is designed to do. We might say, therefore, that, in the two hemispheres of the human brain, there is an echo of the problem/mystery distinction which does not silence other dimensions – scientific/imaginative or artistic/creative – of our search for understanding. These various aspects of reality are not in opposition or conflict with each other. They invite us to view reality from many sides. The simplest example of this is in our two eyes. Each eye views the same scene, but from two slightly different angles. These two views are united, thus enabling us to see the scene with a depth that one eye alone could not achieve. Something similar is the case when we view something with the eye of science and with the eye of faith. Pope Francis says:

> The gaze of science thus benefits from faith: faith encourages the scientist to remain constantly open to reality in all its inexhaustible richness. Faith awakens the critical sense by preventing research from being satisfied with its own formulae and helps it to realize that creation is always greater than our understanding of it. By stimulating wonder before the profound mystery of creation, faith broadens the horizons of reason to shed greater light on the world which discloses itself to scientific investigation.[5]

We may see an example of this mutual enrichment in one of the most spectacular displays of nature – the explosion of colour that is seen most remarkably in the autumn leaves in New England and is seen occasionally, less spectacularly and more briefly, in an Irish autumn. The scientific explanation is that the colours are potentially there all the time, but, during spring and summer the leaves are green because the leaves manufacture nutrients necessary for the growth of the tree. This process takes place in leaves that are rich in chlorophyll, which has a green colour. When autumn comes, because of shorter days and colder temperatures this food-making process ceases and the chlorophyll breaks down, the green colour largely disappears and the orange, red, brown and yellow colours become vibrantly visible. This scientific explanation is true, interesting, even fascinating. There is however another question: 'why does this phenomenon take our breath away?' Science tells us accurately how things happen, but gazing at the splendour of the Shenandoah Valley in the autumn, we have an experience of beauty that touches something deeper in ourselves. Science can explain how this happens, but our recognition of beauty raises other questions within us.

Archbishop Emeritus Chaput of Philadelphia gives an example of how science and faith work together. A friend of his told him how she met God. One night, when she was four or five years old, her father told her to look at the sky and to see the carpet of thousands of stars. He said to her, 'God made the world beautiful because he loves us'.

The Archbishop makes the point that though that was more than fifty years ago, and though his friend grew up and learned all about entropy and supernovae and colliding galaxies and quantum mechanics and the general theory of relativity, the fact is that still, when she closes her eyes, she can see that carpet of stars and hear her father's voice: 'God made the world beautiful because he loves us.'[6]

CHAPTER NINE

Spreading the Joy of the Gospel Together

Pope Francis says that every Christian should be a missionary. It's a demanding call in a busy world where people often feel overburdened: 'How can I be a missionary when my work, my family and my social involvements leave me permanently under pressure, with no spare time in which to be a missionary?' The call can be obscured by busyness but also by an attitude that has developed over the centuries, among both laity and clergy – an attitude which would say, 'leave the task of fulfilling the missionary work of the Church to bishops, priests and religious. That's their job! That's what they are trained to do!' In his address in Limerick in 1979, St John Paul II stressed how mistaken that attitude is. 'There is no such thing as an "ordinary layperson"', he said, 'for all of you have been called to conversion through the death and Resurrection of Jesus Christ. As God's holy people you are called to fulfil your role in the evangelization of the world.'[1]

Pope Francis often says that the Church must be synodal. In a document prepared by the International Theological Commission on Synodality in the life and mission of the Church, we read:

> 'Synod' is an ancient and venerable word in the Tradition of
> the Church, whose meaning draws on the deepest themes of
> Revelation. Composed of a Greek preposition *syn* (with) and the
> noun *odos* (path) it indicates the path along which the People of
> God walk with one another. Equally, it refers to the Lord Jesus,
> who presents Himself as 'the way, the truth and the life' (Jn 14:6),
> and to the fact that Christians, His followers, were originally called
> 'followers of the Way' (cf. Acts 9:2; 19:9, 23; 22:4; 24:14, 22).[2]

Synodality means that the People of God 'walk together' along the way which is Jesus himself. Pope Francis does not see that walking together as a tedious imposition which would distract us from real life. On the contrary, he says:

> The Gospel offers us the chance to live life on a higher plane,
> but with no less intensity: 'Life grows by being given away, and
> it weakens in isolation and comfort. Indeed, those who enjoy
> life most are those who leave security on the shore and become
> excited by the mission of communicating life to others'. When the
> Church summons Christians to take up the task of evangelization,
> she is simply pointing to the source of authentic personal
> fulfilment. For 'here we discover a profound law of reality: that
> life is attained and matures in the measure that it is offered up in
> order to give life to others. This is certainly what mission means'.
> Consequently, an evangelizer must never look like someone who
> has just come back from a funeral![3]

The person who seeks the Good News and seeks to communicate it, opens him or herself to a new level of communication with the ultimate truth and with the source of unlimited joy. Saint John Paul II wrote:

> the more [people] grow in the knowledge of God, the more
> [they] perceive him as an inaccessible mystery, whose essence

> cannot be grasped. This should not be confused with an obscure mysticism in which a person loses himself in enigmatic, impersonal realities. On the contrary, the Christians of the East turn to God as Father, Son and Holy Spirit, living persons tenderly present, to whom they utter a solemn and humble, majestic and simple liturgical doxology. But they perceive that one draws close to this presence above all by letting oneself be taught an adoring silence, for at the culmination of the knowledge and experience of God is God's absolute transcendence. This is reached through the prayerful assimilation of scripture and the liturgy more than by systematic meditation.[4]

The Polish pope and saint was attracted to the Eastern attitude of prayer and their theological method that focused on humbly recognising our limits before the infinite transcendence of the Triune God. He saw it as a gift the East continues to offer all believers in Christ.

> We must confess that we all have need of this silence, filled with the presence of him who is adored: in theology, so as to exploit fully its own sapiential and spiritual soul; in prayer, so that we may never forget that seeing God means coming down the mountain with a face so radiant that we are obliged to cover it with a veil (cf. Ex 34:33), and that our gatherings may make room for God's presence and avoid self-celebration; in preaching, so as not to delude ourselves that it is enough to heap word upon word to attract people to the experience of God; in commitment, so that we will refuse to be locked in a struggle without love and forgiveness. This is what man needs today; he is often unable to be silent for fear of meeting himself, of feeling the emptiness that asks itself about meaning; man who deafens himself with noise. All, believers and non-believers alike, need to learn a silence that allows the Other to speak when and how he wishes, and allows us to understand his words.[5]

CHAPTER TEN

Waiting for What?

Advances in science, engineering, medicine and the analysis of what enables societies to develop for the benefit of their people can bring great advances to human well-being. But they do not offer the fulfilment of all the dreams and hopes of the human heart. Those dreams and hopes point to the finally satisfying destination for human life, described in the familiar words of St Augustine: 'Our delight is to praise you, for you have so made us that we long for you, and our heart is restless until it rests in you.'[1]

Those words of St Augustine point us to the most profound understanding of the question, 'What are we waiting for?' It is our nature as human beings to be people who wait, people who are longing, though we do not always recognise it, for the only destination that can finally satisfy our restless hearts – to rest in the overwhelming love, mercy, beauty, truth and goodness of God who so made us that we would long for him and so that our hearts are restless until we rest in our Creator. That rest will never come to us through wealth or power or through any achievement of skill or knowledge or ingenuity that we may feel pleased about.

Resting in the ever-loving heart of God is a gift beyond anything we can imagine. Yet it is a homecoming. It is a coming back to what our deepest self has always sought. God made us so that we would long for him and so that our longing would be fulfilled when we are in the presence of God who brought each human being into existence and whose Son, Jesus, said: 'I go and prepare a place for you, I will come again and will take you to myself, that where I am you may be also' (Jn 14:3).

In the *Catechism of the Catholic Church* we read how the Church 'teaches that every spiritual soul is created immediately by God – it is not "produced" by the parents – and also that it is immortal: it does not perish when it separates from the body at death, and it will be reunited with the body'.[2] We have been brought into existence by the inexhaustible love of God. The coming into existence of every human life is the beginning of a relationship with God. As we saw in chapter four, Pope Benedict XVI speaks of the memory of our origin that lies within each of us. Something like an original memory of what is good and true has been implanted in us and so there is 'an inner ontological tendency within [the human being], who is created in the likeness of God, toward the divine'.[3]

Jesus spoke to his disciples at the Last Supper about their life's journey towards their divine home:

> 'Let not your hearts be troubled; believe in God, believe also in me.
> In my Father's house are many rooms; if it were not so, would I have told you that I go to prepare a place for you? And when I go and prepare a place for you, I will come again and will take you to myself, that where I am you may be also. And you know the way where I am going.
>
> Thomas said to him, 'Lord, we do not know where you are going; how can we know the way?' Jesus said to him, 'I am the

> way, and the truth, and the life; no one comes to the Father, but
> by me. If you had known me, you would have known my Father
> also; henceforth you know him and have seen him.' (Jn 14:3–5)

I have already referred to St John Paul II's comments on how human beings can find the deepest meaning of our lives in a deep wonder and amazement at who we are in the light of the Gospel. It is now worth listening again, this time to a fuller extract of this powerful passage:

> The person who wishes to understand himself thoroughly – and
> not just in accordance with immediate, partial, often superficial,
> and even illusory standards and measures of his being – he
> must with his unrest, uncertainty and even his weakness and
> sinfulness, with his life and death, draw near to Christ. He must
> … assimilate the whole of the reality of the Incarnation and
> Redemption in order to find himself. If this profound process
> takes place within him, he then bears fruit not only of adoration
> of God but also of deep wonder at himself … In reality, the
> name for that deep amazement at human worth and dignity
> is the Gospel, that is to say: the Good News. It is also called
> Christianity.[4]

That deep amazement points to a goal that is beyond our power to create. David Walsh writes about philosopher and social reformer John Stuart Mill:

> after working for decades on schemes for social improvement
> and political liberalization … he woke up one morning to ask
> himself a simple question: If all that I have been struggling to
> bring about for all these years were suddenly to come true and
> my dream of social transformation were to be realized, would I be
> happy? To his astonishment, he found that the answer that welled

> up spontaneously was No! His work had all been structured by
> the proposition that it could never finally be completed. All of
> the zest and interest it held for him as a human being arose out of
> the security that it was surrounded by a horizon of mystery that
> constantly beckoned him but could never be surpassed.[5]

The achievements of science and technology, our growing knowledge of the universe and our ability to cure illnesses and lethal diseases, are remarkable. But the greatest successes will never finally still the restlessness of human hearts.

Our science, our achievements, our efforts can never fulfil the longing that is in us from the memory of our origin, from God's invitation to us to share in his infinite love, infinite truth, infinite beauty. That original memory is not some alien imposition; it is the key to our own being and our own destiny. It is the heart of who we are. A human being 'hears its echo from within[and] sees: "That's it! That is what my nature points to and seeks."'[6] That echo awakens the mystery which is the source of the restlessness that can find rest only in the Creator.

When Gabriel Marcel said that mystery cannot be understood as an item to be analysed and tested on a laboratory table as if it were a scientific problem (see chapter six), he was pointing out that we cannot stand detached from the mystery of our own lives and our destiny in order to view these questions as if they were a problem quite separate from ourselves to be analysed and solved. The ultimate truth and mystery about ourselves cannot be reached by a detached, neutral reflection. That truth is at the heart of who we are; it echoes in ourselves. When we recognise that truth, we know; or perhaps begin to glimpse, that it is the deepest truth in us: 'That's it! That's what our nature points to and seeks.'

CHAPTER ELEVEN

Resurrection and Ultimate Meaning

Any reflection on the meaning of our lives has to face the most obvious reality: the only absolutely certain fact about every human life is that it will end in death. The person we referred to in the anecdote recounted in chapter seven who described the Resurrection of Christ as 'the most amazing thing' recognised the core of Christian faith. Saint Paul expressed it uncompromisingly: 'For if the dead are not raised, then Christ has not been raised. If Christ has not been raised, our faith is futile and we are still in our sins' (1 Cor 15:16–17). We may indeed be touched by the story of the person's amazement at reading about the Resurrection, but perhaps we should be even more struck by his question: 'Why did you not tell us?'

In his 2016 Easter homily, entitled 'The Disturbing Fact of the Resurrection', Bishop Robert Barron provided an eloquent testimony:

> The resurrection of Jesus from the dead is the be-all and the end-all of the Christian faith. If Jesus didn't rise from the dead, all bishops, priests, and Christian ministers should go home and get honest jobs, and all the Christian faithful should leave their churches immediately. As Paul himself put it: 'If Jesus is

not raised from the dead, our preaching is in vain and we are the most pitiable of men.' It's no good, of course, trying to explain the resurrection away or rationalize it as a myth, a symbol, or an inner subjective experience. None of that does justice to the novelty and sheer strangeness of the biblical message. It comes down finally to this: if Jesus was not raised from death, Christianity is a fraud and a joke; if he did rise from death, then Christianity is the fullness of God's revelation, and Jesus must be the absolute centre of our lives. There is no third option'.[1]

The word 'disturbing' is apt in a culture which is sceptical and dismissive of miracles:

the modern world has a hard time with the Resurrection, and in general with miracles and everything supernatural. At least since the nineteenth century (or perhaps this phenomenon has always been there since we left Eden) the Western mind in particular has been on a campaign of demythologising the faith preached by the Apostles. We read our Bibles like good psychologists, trying to extract some bit of ethical or life wisdom from the stories, but not taking seriously the miracles that are so clearly proclaimed.[2]

That discomfort with miracles is a consequence of what we have already referred to as 'scientism' (see chapter six). Ruling out miracles and, in particular, denying the Resurrection of Jesus Christ is an unequivocal rejection of the central truth of Christian faith. It is of course true that the Resurrection goes beyond all human expectations and assumptions, but that is precisely the point. It is also the central truth of human existence. It is the renewal of all creation. The Book of Revelation says:

I saw the holy city, new Jerusalem, coming down out of heaven from God, prepared as a bride adorned for her husband; and I heard a loud voice from the throne saying, 'Behold, the dwelling

> of God is with men. He will dwell with them, and they shall be his people, and God himself will be with them. He will wipe away every tear from their eyes, and death shall be no more, neither shall there be mourning nor crying nor pain any more, for the former things have passed away.' And he who sat upon the throne said, 'Behold, I make all things new.' (Rv 21:2–5)

We might be tempted to think that the passing away of former things and making everything new would imply the abandonment of scientific knowledge and the fruits of scientific research and a refusal to respect the achievements of human ingenuity in research and innovation; it may be seen as moving into an alien world in which those things no longer matter. On the contrary, we will see all these more clearly and rejoice in them. The *Catechism of the Catholic Church* speaks of how God the Father, 'through his Son Jesus Christ, will pronounce the final word on all history':

> We shall know the ultimate meaning of the whole work of creation and of the entire economy of salvation, and understand the marvellous ways in which his Providence led everything to its final end. The Last Judgement will reveal that God's Justice triumphs over all the injustices committed by his creatures and that God's love is stronger than death.[3]

What we are waiting for with eager longing transcends all the tensions and incomprehension that can arise between mysteries and problems, between the scientific method and the contemplation that gives rise to the wonder and awe at ourselves and at God, our Creator, which, as St John Paul II said, is Christianity, and is the Gospel.[4] The ultimate meaning of the whole work of creation will recognise the different perspectives that arise in our search for the true, the good and the beautiful. It will allow us to understand that, as is the case with our eyes, the merging of these perspectives will allow us to see everything with a depth and clarity that we would never have imagined. As the *Catechism* puts it, 'The manifold perfections of creatures – their truth, their goodness, their beauty – all reflect the infinite perfection of God.'[5]

CHAPTER TWELVE

A New Heaven and a New Earth

The Resurrection of Christ, 'the most amazing thing', is the beginning of something new: 'Christ has been raised from the dead, *the first fruits* of those who have fallen asleep' (1 Cor 15:20). Saint Paul comments on the Resurrection:

> For as by a man came death, by a man has come also the
>   resurrection of the dead.
> For as in Adam all die, so also in Christ shall all be made alive. But
> each in his own order:
> Christ the first fruits, then at his coming those who
>   belong to Christ.
> Then comes the end, when he delivers the kingdom to God the
>   Father after destroying every rule and every authority
>   and power.
> For he must reign until he has put all his enemies under his feet.
> The last enemy to be destroyed is death. (1 Cor 15:21–26)

Words such as 'then comes the end' may arouse a sense of fear. We may remember the account in St Matthew's Gospel of the separation of the sheep and the goats and the casting of the latter into eternal fire. But that judgement repeats a truth we have always known. As Karl Rahner wrote:

> The judgement of God will uncover the hidden recesses of our heart and will confound mere introspection while our heart will admit that at bottom it always knew what now comes to light.[1]

In other words, in the light of God's infinite truth, love and beauty, we will see the truth about ourselves more truly and surely than ever before. Seeing ourselves as we really are will be painful, but what we call purgatory is not just a fire of punishment. Pope Benedict XVI has written:

> Some recent theologians are of the opinion that the fire which both burns and saves is Christ himself, the Judge and Saviour. The encounter with him is the decisive act of judgement. Before his gaze all falsehood melts away. This encounter with him, as it burns us, transforms and frees us, allowing us to become truly ourselves.[2]

The late John Polkinghorne, an Anglican priest and scientist put it like this:

> The concept of judgement as the painful encounter with reality in which all masks of illusion are swept away, is powerful and convincing. It is also basically a hopeful image, for it is only in the recognition and acknowledgement of reality that there can reside the hope of salvation.[3]

But the most fundamental truth that will emerge from the recesses of our hearts is not our sins. It will be our wonder and amazement at the unlimited love of God who brought us into existence and sent his Son to be our way and truth and life, even to sacrificing himself on a cross for us, and sustained us throughout the journey of our lives. We will recognise the unlimited love that leads us into the new creation.

Some years before he was elected pope, Cardinal Ratzinger wrote a book with the title *Eschatology: Death and Eternal Life*. He reflected in depth on the meaning of resurrection. In particular, he wrote about the immortality of the soul. The human soul is immortal, though not as a result of its accomplishments or qualities or resources:

> It is not a relationless 'being oneself' that makes the human being immortal, but precisely his/her relationship or capacity for relatedness to God. We must now add that such an opening of one's existence is not a trimming, an addition to a being that really might exist in an independent fashion. On the contrary, it constitutes what is deepest in man's being. It is nothing other than what we call 'soul'.[4]

There is, as we already noted (see chapter four), deep within us an original memory of the beginning of that relationship with our Creator. That there is such a relationship at the origin of each human life is a fundamental teaching of the Catholic Church. Pope Pius XII, echoing the Fifth Lateran Council said: 'The Catholic faith obliges us to hold that souls are immediately created by God.'[5] In the prophet Jeremiah we read, 'Before I formed you in the womb I knew you, and before you were born I consecrated you' (Jer 1:5).

That relationship is an act of God's always-reliable love. In one of Gabriel Marcel's plays a character says, 'To love a being is to say, you, you in particular will never die.'[6] Such a never-ending relationship begins when God establishes an eternal relationship with every human being. In that moment, God is saying to each human soul: 'you will never die'.

That hope is there also for the relationships of love that we have with each other. The funeral service addresses those who are present with these words:

> My brothers and sisters, we believe that all the ties of friendship
> and affection which knit us as one throughout our lives do not
> unravel with death. Confident that God remembers all the good
> we have done, and forgives our sins, let us pray, asking God to
> gather all of us together in his kingdom, where every tear will be
> wiped away and all will be made new. Through Christ our Lord.
> Amen.[7]

Cardinal Ratzinger summed up why the human soul is immortal when he wrote, 'Immortality does not inhere in a human being but rests on a relation, on a *relationship* with what is eternal, what makes eternity meaningful. ... [The human being] can, therefore, live for ever, because he is able to have a relationship with that which gives the eternal.'[8]

Saint Thomas Aquinas in his commentary on the final section of the Apostles' Creed offered some reflections on what eternal life will mean:

> everlasting life is the full and perfect satisfying of every desire; for
> there every blessed soul will have to overflowing what he hoped
> for and desired. The reason is that in this life no one can fulfil all
> his desires, nor can any created thing fully satisfy the craving of
> [humankind]. Only God satisfies and infinitely exceeds [human]
> desires ... If knowledge is desired, it will be there most perfectly,
> because we shall possess in the life everlasting the knowledge of
> all the nature of things and of all truth, and whatever we desire we
> shall now possess, that we shall have, even life eternal: 'Now, all
> good things come to me together with her' (Wis 7:11). 'To the
> just their desire shall be given' (Prov 10:24).[9]

Finally, in heaven there will be the happy society of all the blessed, and this society will be especially delightful. Since each one will possess all good together with the blessed, and they will love one another as themselves, and they will rejoice in the others' good as their own. It will also happen that, as the pleasure and enjoyment of one increases, so will it be for all: 'The dwelling in you is as it were of all rejoicing' (Ps 87:7.)

What we are waiting for is all we could wish for, and far more. Although we will also realise that we fell short, perhaps seriously short, in our response to that love, we will be surrounded by a goodness, a beauty and a merciful love that infinitely exceeds all our desires.

What we are waiting for is not just a personal fulfilment. N.T. Wright, former Church of England Bishop of Durham and an eminent scripture scholar, emphasises the importance of seeing the larger picture. The Resurrection is not just about the destiny of individuals. It is about the renewal of all creation. It is about making all things, the whole world, new and he says, 'the point of the Gospels and the Acts of the Apostles is that this renewal of creation has already begun.'[10] He points out that:

> To make any headway in understanding the Eucharist we must see it as the arrival of God's future into our present. We do not simply remember a long-since dead Jesus, we celebrate the presence of the living Lord … The Jesus who gives himself to us as food and drink is himself the beginning of God's new world. At communion we are like the children of Israel in the wilderness, tasting fruit plucked from the promised land. It is the future coming to meet the present.[11]

What our world is waiting for? This has been a question running throughout my short work. In his work on hope, Bishop Wright provides words that express a key faith-filled conviction I have wanted to open up for readers: 'What creation needs is neither abandonment nor evolution but rather redemption and renewal; and this is both promised and guaranteed by the resurrection of Jesus from the dead. This is what the whole world's waiting for.'[12]

ENDNOTES

....

INTRODUCTION

1   See Donal Murray, *Picking up the Shards*, Dublin: Veritas, 2019, p.11.

2   Cardinal Francis George OMI, 'The Wrong Side of History', *Chicago Catholic*, 21 October 2012. https://www.chicagocatholic.com/cardinal-george/-/article/2012/10/21/the-wrong-side-of-history; accessed on 12 August 2021.

3   Benedict XVI, General Audience, 27 January 2010. https://www.vatican.va/content/benedict-xvi/en/audiences/2010/documents/hf_ben-xvi_aud_20100127.html; accessed on 12 August 2021.

4   Cf. Francis, *Evangelii Gaudium*, *passim*, especially 119 ff.

5   Enzo Farinella, 'Europe and the Irish Monks'. http://www.saint-brendan.org/news.asp?p=europe-and-the-irish-monks-by-enzo-farinella; accessed on 12 December 2018.

6   Thomas Cahill, *How the Irish Saved Civilization*, New York: Doubleday, 1995, p. 196.

7   Francis, *Evangelii Gaudium*, 120.

8   Address of his Holiness Benedict XVI Meeting with Representatives from the World of Culture, Collège des Bernardins, Paris, 12 September 2008. https://www.vatican.va/content/benedict-xvi/en/speeches/2008/september/documents/hf_ben-xvi_spe_20080912_parigi-cultura.html; accessed on 12 August 2021.

9   Cardinal Robert Sarah, interview by Edward Pentin, *National Catholic Register*: http://www.ncregister.com/daily-news/cardinal-sarahs-cri-de-coeur-the-catholic-church-has-lost-its-sense-of-the-sacred; accessed on 23 September 2019.

10   John Paul II, *Centesimus Annus*, 24; cf. also *Centesimus Annus*, 13.

11   Joseph Ratzinger, *L'Europa di Benedetto nella crisi delle culture*, Siena: Cantagalli, 2005. pp. 63–4. Cf. Stanisław Ryłko, *Pontifical Council for the Laity News Bulletin* 22, 2011, available at https://www.vatican.va/roman_curia/pontifical_councils/laity/laity_en/pubblicazioni/rc_pc_laity_doc_20120326_notiziario-22-2011_en.html; accessed 12 August 2021.

12   Address of his Holiness Pope Francis to Students, Fr Felix Varela Cultural Centre, Havana, 20 September 2015.

CHAPTER ONE: HOW CAN WE KNOW THE WAY?

1   Cf. Augustine, *Confessions*, 1:1.

2   Cf. Columbanus, *Instructiones*, XI.

3   Benedict XVI, General Audience, 11 June 2008. https://www.vatican.va/content/benedict-xvi/en/audiences/2008/documents/hf_ben-xvi_aud_20080611.html; accessed on 12 August 2021.

4   Ibid.

5   See Francis, *Fratelli Tutti*.

6   William Shakespeare, *Hamlet*, Act 3, Scene 1.

7   'Eucharistic Prayer for Use in Masses for Various Needs III', *The Roman Missal*, Dublin: Veritas, 2011, p. 673.

8   www.carmelitesofboston.org/prayer/prayers-of-carmelite-saints/st-therese-of-the-child-jesus-and-the-holy-face; original italics removed; accessed on 12 August 2021.

9   *Catechism of the Catholic Church*, 2855.

Endnotes

CHAPTER TWO: A MISSIONARY JOURNEY

1   John P. Jordan C.S.Sp., *Bishop Shanahan of Southern Nigeria*, Dublin: Clonmore and Reynolds, 1949, p. 186.

2   Jean-Baptiste Chautard, *The Soul of the Apostolate*, North Carolina: TAN Books, St Benedict's Press, 2012, p. 165.

3   John Paul II, Homily at Holy Mass in Limerick, 1 October 1979. https://www.vatican.va/content/john-paul-ii/en/homilies/1979/documents/hf_jp-ii_hom_19791001_irlanda-limerick.html; accessed on 12 August 2021.

4   Francis, *Evangelii Gaudium*, 120.

5   Benedict XVI, *Spe Salvi*, 2.

6   Ibid.

7   Benedict XVI, *Sacramentum Caritatis*, 84.

CHAPTER THREE: THE WAY OF WONDER

1   Paul VI, *Evangelii Nuntiandi*, 41.

2   From a sermon by St Gregory Nazianzen, *Oration 14: On Love of the Poor*, https://anastpaul.wordpress.com/2019/03/11/lenten-thoughts-11-march-let-us-show-each-other-gods-generosity-saint-gregory-nazianzen-330-390/; accessed on 29 April 2019.

3   John Paul II, *Redemptor Hominis*, 10.

4   John Paul II, *Fides et Ratio*, 1.

CHAPTER FOUR: THE MEMORY OF OUR ORIGIN

1   Joseph Ratzinger, 'Conscience and Truth', Presented at the 10th Workshop for Bishops, Dallas, Texas, February 1991. https://www.ewtn.com/catholicism/library/conscience-and-truth-2468; accessed on 19 March 2021.

2   Ibid.

3   Pius XII, *Humani generis*: DS 3896; Lateran Council V (1513): DS 1440.

4   Robert W. Service, 'The Spell of the Yukon', *The Spell of the Yukon and Other Verses*, New York: Barse & Hopkins, 1907, courtesy of Anne Longépé, Robert W. Service's estate.

5   Cf. John Paul II, *Redemptor Hominis*, 10; see page 29 of this volume.

6   Second Vatican Council, *Constitution on the Sacred Liturgy: Sacrosanctum Concilium*, Vatican City: Libreria Editrice Vaticana, 1963, 33.

7   Benedict XVI, Inaugural Address to 5th General Conference of Latin American and Caribbean Bishops, 13 May 2007. https://www.vatican.va/content/benedict-xvi/en/speeches/2007/may/documents/hf_ben-xvi_spe_20070513_conference-aparecida.html; accessed on 12 August 2021.

CHAPTER FIVE: IT'S NOT ABOUT STATISTICS

1   Pastoral Letter of the Holy Father, Pope Benedict XVI, to the Catholics of Ireland, 19 March 2010. https://www.vatican.va/content/benedict-xvi/en/letters/2010/documents/hf_ben-xvi_let_20100319_church-ireland.html; accessed on 12 August 2021.

2   Benedict XVI, Address at Collège des Bernardins, Paris, 12 September 2008.

3   Gabriel Marcel, *Homo Viator*, New York: Harper Torchbooks, 1962, p. 160.

CHAPTER SIX: LET US NOT SEEK EN ROUTE WHAT WE
                  SHALL BE IN OUR HOMELAND

1   See Tomás Ó Fiaich, *Columbanus in His Own Words*, Dublin: Veritas, 1974, p. 90, quoting Columbanus, Sermon V on eternal life.

2   Gabriel Marcel, *Mystery of Being*, vol. 1, Chicago: Gateway, 1960, p. 260.

3   John Paul II, *Fides et Ratio*, 88.

4   Marcel, *Mystery of Being*, p. 260.

5   See Archbishop Joseph E. Kurtz, 'Teaching our Faith – Faith and Science' in *The Record* (1 May 2019). https://therecordnewspaper.org/teaching-our-faith-faith-and-science/; accessed on 28 March 2021.

Endnotes

CHAPTER SEVEN: THE MOST AMAZING THING

1 Benedict XVI, Address at the Collège des Bernardins, Paris, 12 September 2008.
2 Benedict XVI, 'Faith, Reason and the University – Memories and Reflections', University of Regensbury, 12 September 2006.
3 John Paul II, *Fides et Ratio*, 1.

CHAPTER EIGHT: BOTH/AND

1 Patricia Kieran, 'Striving for the Attainable? Creative Religious Education and Catechesis', in *The Pastoral Review*, May/June (2012), pp. 33–38.
2 Benedict XVI, Address at the University of Regensburg, 12 September 2006.
3 Iain McGilchrist, *The Master and his Emissary: The Divided Brain and the Making of the Western World*, New Haven: Yale University Press, 2009, p. 23.
4 Ibid.
5 Francis, *Laudato Si'*, footnote 141.
6 Charles J. Chaput, *Strangers in a Strange Land: Living the Catholic Faith in a Post-Christian World*, New York: Henry Holt and Company, 2017.

CHAPTER NINE: SPREADING THE JOY OF THE GOSPEL TOGETHER

1 John Paul II, Homily at Mass in Limerick, Ireland, 1 October 1979.
2 International Theological Commission, *Synodality in the life and mission of the Church*, 2018. http://www.vatican.va/roman_curia/congregations/cfaith/cti_documents/rc_cti_20180302_sinodalita_en.html; accessed on 12 August 2021.
3 Francis, *Evangelii Gaudium*, 10.
4 John Paul II, Apostolic Letter, *Orientale Lumen*, n. 16.
5 Ibid.

CHAPTER TEN: WAITING FOR WHAT?

1 St Augustine, *Confessions*, translated Benignus O'Rourke OSA, London: Darton, Longman and Todd, 2013, Book 1, Ch. 1.

2 *Catechism of the Catholic Church*, 366.

3 See Joseph Ratzinger, 'Conscience and Truth', presented at the 10th Workshop for Bishops, Dallas, Texas, February 1991. https://www.ewtn.com/catholicism/library/conscience-and-truth-2468; accessed on 19 March 2021.

4 John Paul II, *Redemptor Hominis*, 10.

5 David Walsh, *Guarded by Mystery*, Washington D.C.: The Catholic University of America Press, 1999, pp. 13-14.

6 Ratzinger, 'Conscience and Truth'; see Chapter Four of this volume.

CHAPTER ELEVEN: RESURRECTION AND ULTIMATE MEANING

1 Robert Barron, 'The Disturbing Fact of The Ressurrection', https://www.wordonfire.org/resources/article/the-disturbing-fact-of-the-resurrection/5119/; accessed on 19 March 2021.

2 David A. Smither, 'Why So Many People Don't Want to Believe in the Resurrection', *National Catholic Register*, 26 April 2020.

3 *Catechism of the Catholic Church*, 1040–1041.

4 Cf. John Paul II, *Redemptor Hominis*, 10; see page 29 of this volume.

5 Ibid., 41.

CHAPTER TWELVE: A NEW HEAVEN AND A NEW EARTH

1 Karl Rahner, *On Prayer*, Collegeville: Liturgical Press, 1993, p. 113.

2 Benedict XVI, *Spe Salvi*, 47. This is a typically humble reference by Pope Benedict XVI: one of those theologians is himself: cf. Ratzinger, *Eschatology: Death and Eternal Life*, Aidan Nichols O.P. (trans.), Washington DC: Catholic University of America Press, 1988, p. 229.

3 John Polkinghorne, *The God of Hope and the End of the World*, New Haven: Yale University Press, 2003, p. 131.

4 Ratzinger, *Eschatology*, p. 155.

Endnotes

5   Pope Pius XII, *Humani Generis*, 36.

6   Gabriel Marcel, *Homo Viator*, New York: Harper Torchbooks, 1962, p. 147.

7   Cf. *Order of Christian Funerals*, Dublin: Veritas, 2015, p. 36.

8   Ratzinger, *Eschatology*, p. 259.

9   Thomas Aquinas, 'The Carechetical Instructions of St Thomas', https://www.ewtn.com/catholicism/library/catechetical-instructions-of-st-thomas-12543; accessed on 4 June 2020.

10   N.T. Wright, *Surprised by Hope: Rethinking Heaven, the Resurrection, and the Mission of the Church*, New York: Harper Collins, 2018, p. 201.

11   Ibid., p. 274.

12   Ibid., p. 107.

Dancing With The Juggler

Thirteen Moons With the Tarot and Natural Magic

by Carolynn Clare Townsend

www.capallbann.co.uk

Dancing With The Juggler

Thirteen Moons With the Tarot and Natural Magic

ISBN 186163 123 5

Cover design by Paul Mason
Internal illustrations by Carolynn Clare Townsend

Published by:

Capall Bann Publishing
Freshfields
Chieveley
Berks
RG20 8TF

Dedication

For my King of Pentacles and Knight of Cups, with love

Contents

The Fool

Introduction

This is a practical, 'how to' book; a year's course, month by season, festivals and days, on using the Tarot and what has become known as ' natural magic' to develop your own intuitive and spiritual energies and change your life.

Hang on! Yes, I know 'change your life' made you want to put this back on the shelf but - listen.

Because of the work I do, I was often told by my students or clients that 'you must read this book! It changed my life!' They would then lend me the book and I'd read a few chapters, yawn a bit, and politely return it. There are so many books on how to change your life, live in higher consciousness, get thin, get beautiful, have it all. If these books worked, how jolly everything would be, wouldn't it, with the world full of love and positive people leaping about doing everything they always wanted. But it isn't.

One day, one of my students lent me a book I'd heard of several times in this way and she insisted I should read it, so I took it to bed with me the night before she was due for her next lesson, read three chapters; and it really was just the same 'think positively, focus on what you want' formula. I went to sleep. In the middle of the night I woke suddenly, and my High Priestess image was clear in my head, in all the vibrant colours I painted her almost thirty years ago when I made my own Tarot pack. In my deck, I designed her holding a book - the book of knowledge; a book of shadows, if you will, which holds the secrets of the universe.

In my 'waking dream' my High Priestess picked up the book and threw it at me.

It was a manuscript, and I thought I knew exactly what she meant.

I turned over and settled down to go back to sleep. She had to be joking.

My Lady, I told her sleepily, I've had enough of writing books.

Oh, yes.

*

Ever since I can remember I've been a writer. Little books of stories stapled together when I was small, long letters to penfriends, then later, short stories, the teenage poems, then the serious stuff. Months on chapters for all sorts of proposals. Mills and Boon, the local writers' clubs, Black Lace. Articles. Anyone who loves - has - to write will know what I mean.

One day, the impossible happened and a publishing company wanted my first completed book.

I was on another planet for seven days, and then the whole thing fell through. The story of why and what isn't important - but the horrible pit of despair into which it plunged me is intrinsic to this book. After I'd given up any notion of becoming a bestseller overnight, I continued with my life. But it had changed.

*

Because of the way my life changed - and since it started with such desperation at a disappointment - I wasn't aware of it at first. I fell back on my work, my friends and my personal spiritual way because I felt sorry for myself, and because I didn't want to touch the word processor.

I wasn't going to write another *thing* - **nothing**, so there. I would do anything but write another book.

I began to observe the festivals with more concentration.

I was initiated into one of the quasi-Gardenerian witchcraft groups in the late sixties; but I was much too young, and too many other things were happening then for me to pay proper attention to my spiritual life. So, I had to learn the hard way, and I came back to the Old Gods after denying them their respect for far too long. I needed to start all over again. But as soon as I did, my world began to change.

It wasn't a sudden thing, and it won't be with you. You don't need to be already into natural magic, witchcraft (all of it done properly is 'white' incidentally - but more of that later) to use Tarot cards to help change things. (There is even a Christian-inspired deck.- gods help us!) Most other religions find no problem at all with the Tarot.

All you need to do is give this book a year - thirteen moons, four seasons. Read it through completely to begin with. Then start with the next season, or festival, after you decide to follow this course. You buy, or perhaps you already own some Tarot cards - and you promise yourself that life will improve. That's all. No funny words, no weirdness, no hype, no lies.

Natural magic is exactly what it says. Natural - to you, to other people, to the world, to the universe - and to the being or beings we worship, however we perceive them.

This book, like the Tarot and life itself, is cyclic. You start the course at the time of year you wish. If you buy this book in

August, ignore the first chapters after you've read it through and go straight to August - you'll be beginning with Lammas. The wheel of the year is just that, a wheel. It doesn't matter when you get on, but you should follow the thirteen moons through.

We will be concentrating on the major Arcana of the Tarot, which is 22 cards, and we'll be investigating one or two each month.

The minor Arcana - the 4 suits of 14 cards each - are dealt with in a separate chapter, and their meanings are at the end of the book along with the accepted, 'sound byte' meanings of the major Arcana which are easy to learn, and which are designed as triggers for the more complex meanings you'll be able to learn more at your leisure, and while actually practising. (See appendix, 'The Meanings of the Minor Arcana').

If you glance through this book, you'll be able to recognise Tarot cards. If you follow the course through, you'll be able after a year to read them intuitively, and you will have developed your spirituality so that your personal life - I promise you - will have taken on a new meaning.

This is not just a book on how to read Tarot cards. Anybody can buy a pack and the little book that goes with it. Doing that is not reading the Tarot successfully, as anyone who has tried such a method will know. This book will show you what the Tarot really means - and to understand that, you have to let it change your life by helping it to change your perception.

The Tarot has a lot to do with balance - during your first tentative readings for yourself you'll find Justice appearing time and again, regardless of how you shuffle and cut your cards. It always does. The cards are amazing because they will always seek to address the imbalance in the area of the life of the querant as they see it. The Tarot is also always optimistic. Newcomers to my practice sometimes say 'You won't tell me anything bad, will you?' Well, of course I won't . That isn't how the Tarot works at all.

The Tarot is a counsel, a giver of options; and because it's working for you as the querant it's going to try to help, rather than giving out gloom. The cards want to tell you how to better your life; not that people are going to drop dead all around you.

They also can be, in the right hands, very specific indeed. I have to show my hand here and say that I am not a lover of so-called 'Psychic Fairs'. If you are - and this is only page eleven so you might be looking through it with a view to buying this book - don't.

It's the lack of any definitive base that makes the Tarot so special. It doesn't belong to anyone. Nobody can claim it. It is, as its own last card proclaims; of The World.

That's why you can use it, whether you are Christian, Muslim, Pagan or simply, as possibly most of us are; a seeker of the truth which we know to be within us but which needs unlocking, freeing, before we can say we honestly know what is certain. We are all - those of us who seek - on the right road. It's just that there are very many junctions, cross-roads and diversions. Not to mention road works.

If you're feeling emotionally challenged, you'll find Cups will dominate your readings.

Pentacles will try to give you help with your security - the material side of your life. Wands will give you insight into new careers, or opportunities for studies and new possibilities.

Swords, the suit of battles, are always looked on with horror by new converts to the Tarot, but when they appear they really should be respected, since they represent the possible solution to problems and possibly an end to struggles the querant has yet to see.

You'll be dancing, in the end, with The Juggler - the card that represents all higher planes of intuitive thought, and all new, confident, positive beginnings.

If you are serious about changing your life and dancing with The Juggler, you have loads of time. You've got the rest of your life. Shall we go for it?

Chapter One

Choosing Your Tarot Deck, and Other Starting Points

Hopefully, you haven't rushed out and bought any old Tarot deck!

The basic thing you need to know right now is how to choose your deck, because there are literally hundreds of different Tarot packs, and I can't stress too much how important it is for you to have the right one for you.

My students range from those who begin without a deck at all; those who have one but are not sure about it being 'right'; those who have in some way been given one; and those who seized on a beautiful deck which spoke to them in a shop and now want to learn what to do with it. Please, everyone, read a) first, even if you've inherited Great -granny's heirloom deck. (Especially if you have.)

a) You don't yet have a Tarot deck

Great! Please, please - for learning, buy a traditional deck. Once you've mastered the basics of Tarot, you'll be able to choose another, perhaps modern or unusual deck that appeals to you. You will find this book easy if you have one of the older decks - Morgan Greer is excellent because the symbolism is easy to learn and it's the one I use for enhancing the deck I made myself, Rider-Waite is another dependable one.

Basically, look for the traditional images and names - The Fool with his animal companion and his pack, The Juggler/Magician with his table on which lie the four suits - pentacles, wands (or rods), cups and swords. Fortitude or Strength should be opening the jaws of a lion. The Hanged Man should be swinging happily by one leg, and traditionally he has blue hair. The Tower should have a storm around it and people falling from it. There should be The Star, The Moon and The Sun. The Wheel of Fortune must be present, as must The Hermit. The four suits should be those named above, and they should be illustrated too - not just pictures of, for example, four pentacles or three cups. Most important of all - there must be High Priestess and Heirophant (sometimes High Priest); Empress and Emperor. If all these are there, the other cards will usually be right for a novice.

Okay, so you've looked through the cards. (If the shop won't let you, don't buy them there. Shops that understand Tarot should have packs you can look at and handle before you buy, or a catalogue showing you the designs.)

The final test is up to you. Do you like them?

One more thing.

Fish out the High Priestess. Look carefully at this card, because she is going to be the key to your next year. Remember - this isn't just about the Tarot. This is about changing you. Do you like her?

Look into the face on the card. Don't be embarrassed - they're just as wary of you as you are of them; which is why you must have the right pack for you.

If you get a 'feeling' - and you'll know if you have - either buy or look again.

Please remember, though - there are some wondrous Tarot packs out there now. If you choose a traditional one just for this year you will hone your intuitive reading skills far more easily and faster, and then be able to adapt to the deck of your choice.

b) You have a Tarot deck but aren't sure if it feels 'right'

Read the above a).

Then, isolate the following cards, in order, and spend a few seconds looking at each. It doesn't matter that you don't know what they mean at the moment. It actually helps if you don't.

High Priestess

Wheel of Fortune

The Moon (if you're female) or The Sun (if you're male)

The Star

Now how do you feel? Warm and excited about your future together with this deck? Or still puzzled? Go with your instinct. In future chapters, I'll explain how to dowse for things like this, but a Tarot deck has to be chosen by instinct. If you still can't be sure, your pack isn't right for you. Look for another, and go back to a).

c) You've been given, or somehow acquired a Tarot deck

This is quite an interesting situation and it depends very much on the donor of your pack.

It's sometimes the precursor of a very happy partnership with the Tarot, but the rules above still apply. You have to like the images, and, if you're learning, the images must be traditional if you want me to teach you. But - the gift of a Tarot pack is very special, particularly if it's bequeathed. So, to those lucky enough to have been given a deck - if the deck is not a traditional one, keep it very safe and learn as quickly as you can on Morgan Greer or Rider Waite, then transfer your knowledge to your gifted deck.

Here I have to tell a story from one of my students.

Mary's mother-in-law was obviously a talented lady in spiritual realms and she must have recognised the potential in Mary. When she died, she left Mary her Tarot pack in her will, and Mary found it in a drawer during the clearing of the house by her husband and herself. This is a very sad thing to have to do, as anyone who has done it will know, but Mary told me how for some reason she had felt 'buzzy' as she opened the drawer, and that she knew exactly where to look .

She knew nothing about the Tarot, but was intrigued. The pack had one of those 'mini quick meanings' booklets with it, so Mary read it; was confused, and a friend recommended her to me.

Mary's first lesson was a disaster, because although the pack was a traditional one, the High Priestess was missing.. Without the High Priestess, my way of teaching has no basis. We discussed this, and I recognised in Mary - as I suspect her intuitive mother-in-law must have done - a very spiritually aware lady who needed the not so spiritual kick up the arse to propel her out of career woman mode and into look-around-the corner mode. I suggested she draw the High Priestess and ask for guidance from the rest of her cards. Something made her ask one of her young daughters to do the drawing and lo! her husband found the High Priestess in the garden shed.

Now why was it there?

Not actually as barmy as it sounds. I take my High Priestess with me when I go away, and Mary's mother- in- law was a committed gardener. Prince Charles talks to his plants and he's a Christian, allegedly. Pagans are allowed liberties: we can ask guidance from the High Priestess in the potting shed and communicate directly. (It cuts out the need to visit the Garden Centre for advice!)

ð) You were seized with passion for a Tarot deck in a shop

Weren't we all! But you'll have read a). Also, are you sure it wasn't the shop assistant? One of my colleagues, a beautiful lady in her fifties, attracts men quite obliviously wherever we go with her. Museum curators, Stonehenge car park attend-ants, Avebury walkers - all fall for her. She once ran a very successful shop, and she could sell you liar dice and swear they were runes. (She never would, but I use her integrity to prove that some people do.)

It hasn't been unknown for people to be sold very expensive, beautiful Tarot cards which are impossible to learn with because of the lack of any traditional imagery at all. As I keep saying, there are some wonderful decks around but you don't put an eight year old pony lover onto a thoroughbred at Epsom, do you?

This insistence on the traditional would not have been necessary in 1971 when I made my own pack. I made it partly because I was fascinated by what were then quite unusual images, and because I knew intuitively that if I was to work with these things they had to be mine.

I was 21, newly married, and missing the buzz of Art School. My husband was Head of Art at a local high school and we'd moved into a vast, but empty, house away from my childhood village. I was lonely. It was a nice project. .

My father was - and still is - a Healer. He doesn't like the term Faith, or Spiritual healer. He tries to heal all, he says, regardless of whether or not the patient has any faith. I grew up with this attitude, so I was never closed to anything spiritual in any way. It was part of life. If you had a headache, Daddy put his hand on your brow and it went. Until my teens I honestly thought this was what all fathers did. They disappeared on the train in the morning, and came back at night. If you had toothache you went to the dentist, and if you had a fever you were immured under a mountain of blankets to sweat it out. If it didn't get better you went to the doctor's surgery. For any other complaint, didn't everyone have a father like mine? Well, no: but I never realised that.

Similarly, when I picked up a book by Cheiro that my father had bought second-hand during the forties; I didn't realise that it held the key to my future life.

I was about thirteen, and as I read about Palmistry - 'Cheiro' was an oddly charismatic chap who claimed to be a count during the twenties and read the hands of the rich and famous with great success - I was fascinated, and began to absorb his teaching. At first, it was just very interesting. But I'd started on my own pathway. I had yet to see a Tarot pack, but I was The Fool, beginning on my exciting journey into the realms of the spiritual pathway, where things are not always exactly going to happen as you think they are.

There. You have just learned the 'intuitive' meaning of The Fool. Now, when you turn again to the explanations at the back, it makes much more sense, doesn't it?

Chapter Two

Preparing Your Dancefloor

You will need for this chapter:

A compass, or a map of your area, so that you can work out the way your home faces.

Paper and clipboard for notes.

This chapter is aimed at helping you to begin looking at the world in a different way.

Basically, natural magic is concerned with the five elements which govern our planet, and therefore our bodies and our lives. These five elements are:

Earth, Air, Fire, Water and Ether, or Spirit. We are going to cover each of these fully in the chapters which follow, but for now, all you need to know is that each element has its corresponding compass point - except Ether. If you imagine a cross with north and south at the top and bottom respectively, and west on the left and east on the right, Ether is at the centre.

Try the exercises which follow. They can be done any time, any moon, but you should do them before you turn to the chapter heralding your own initiative month. One word - make sure you feel happy with the month you start. It isn't fixed that you start with a particular month. You may buy this book perhaps in July and be on holiday in August. Your birthday may be in January and someone gives you this for Christmas.

First rule of natural magic - go with how it seems right. Read, but don't follow slavishly if you're not happy. If you are drawn to July; wait until July. If you read through February in March and think you can do it - go for it.

But don't skip seasons. You will miss out - honestly, you will.

Exercises

1. Work out the alignment of your own house and garden, if you have one. Draw a simple plan of it and a room or part of a room where you can quietly meditate. (there will always be somewhere.)

2. Then go into this space, being aware of the compass alignments. You are going to learn to instinctively imagine each of the elements in the corners. (The four points of the compass are called 'corners', making the working circle the only round with four corners.)

3. Begin with North. North is the corner which relates to Earth; and is therefore the obvious place to start. Begin by looking North - don't worry if you're facing a blank wall; you soon will know how to make that dissolve. For now, just face North. Concentrate your mind on thinking about what Earth means to you personally. This is called acknowledging the corner, in very simple terms. You could, for example, imagine a wood, or a hill, a field or a garden where you've recently felt especially conscious of the beauty of Nature. Try to remember it in detail, and relive the walk or experience. Close your eyes, if you like (this will help if your North faces a blank wall!)

Become conscious of your heartbeat and your breathing. Match them, in your mind, to your stride as you walk along the favoured, remembered route. Be aware that they will slow to fit in time with your stride.

This should last for two minutes at the very most. If you try to stretch it out you'll get bored at this point in your development. Once your mind shifts to shopping lists or weekend socialising - stop. You've not done this before, and remember you've a year. The Goddess Earth never rushes things, so neither should you.

Now, still facing North, say, or think, something along the lines of:

Spirits of the North, Guardians of Earth, look kindly on me. I am learning every day. Allow me to trust you, and to trust myself to recognise the truth.

Remember - go with your instinct. If other words bubble up in your mind, use them. Concentrate on facing North, thinking about the Earth, our planet, and all it/she means to you. (This will be covered more fully later, in the chapter on Earth)

Now, briefly, you're going to acknowledge and recognise the other three quarters, and then thank the fifth element, Ether or Spirit, for - well - basically for getting you this far! Remember - Ether is the pulse, the key to everything spiritual. You may have a different word for Ether. I call it Spirit - you may call it by the name of your god.

At this point, having acknowledged and asked guidance from North, the other corners are content to add a bit of their wisdom, without you needing to get too involved in circle casting and invoking at this stage. We'll touch on each, just to bring you a taste of the magic of the corners.

So, now move clockwise (deosil). At east, imagine a breeze in your hair. . At south, feel the warmth of the sun; the heat of fire. Very briefly, imagine the raindrops, a waterfall or a river in your mind's eye when you look west. Back at north, be aware of your feet on the ground and the earth below you.

4. Sit, if possible facing north. Place your feet on the ground, (legs and arms uncrossed, because crossing your limbs stops the flow of energy; both psychic and physical) and breath deeply and calmly. After a moment or two, write any thoughts or occurrences down.

It doesn't matter if you've written 'what the **** am I doing?'

You'll get there. Believe me, you will.

Now, when you can, go into your workspace when you feel relaxed and make sure you're not waiting for the phone to ring or the children to burst through the doors. Have a cup of tea, a glass of wine, a fag (if you must!) - personally I love chilled tomato juice before a meditation. Iced, pure water is an obvious favourite, too.

Relax. *Don't think of anything.*

This is going to make you think of everything!

So stop, and try to regulate your breathing this way.

Put one hand just below your diaphragm (about 8cms up from your navel) and breathe in. Does it *do* anything? No?

Okay. Now do it again, and this time consciously make your hand move by trying to fill your diaphragm with air first, before you fill the upper part of your lungs. As you do this, count to ten. Now you should feel your hand move outwards, and you should also feel that you've managed to inhale twice the amount of air that you normally do. Try to hold it for the count of six - this might be difficult at first, so don't worry, it will come - and then breathe out, releasing the air first from the upper part of your lungs, and then feel your hand move inwards as you push the air up from your diaphragm to your mouth - and let it go, if you can, to the count of ten again. Wait six counts, and inhale again.

The first time you do this it will seem the most boring thing on earth. The second and third times you'll see how easy it is. It's really how we're meant to breathe when we're relaxed. It recharges us.

Now, in your comfortable, quiet place, having taking a few deep breaths this way, read the following three sentences. Take a few minutes just to sit quietly and think about each one. Turn them over in your mind. One will probably appeal more than the others. It's meant to.

Try not to think too hard - allow your intuition to make the decision.

a. 'Life is what happens while you're busy making other plans.'

b. 'There is no such thing as coincidence.'

c. 'Send it upstairs.'

Allow your thoughts to wash over the chosen phrase. Repeat it to yourself in your mind, over and over. Then just quietly wait, and see what other thoughts come into your mind. If your mind wanders, repeat the chosen phrase again.

Next time you try this, you'll probably find you choose a different sentence. Try it on different days and at different times, until you have meditated on each, and every time, try to write down something - however apparently meaningless - that occurred to you.

That's the end of the exercises for this chapter. It's been a long set, with the meditation, but deliberately so. Well done. Things will get easier now. You'll gradually learn to enjoy and make space for your meditations, and problems in daily life will present different aspects for you to explore.

I told you this was no ordinary book. The 'answers' to the statements are contained in other chapters. I know that's infuriating, so you have been given clues, and we all love puzzles. Life is one. You're reading this book because you think it may be the answer to yours.

Chapter Three

Put On Your Dancing Shoes

Preparation for first steps with The Juggler - a slow waltz with natural magic

You will need for this chapter:
The High Priestess and The Juggler(Magician)

also (but optional!) One local wild flower or fruit, depending on the season
a glass of water or wine
a joss stick
a red candle
a white candle
this book, this chapter, for reference
a tray to put all the above on

You've learned a little about meditation, and the ability to take your mind somewhere you know and remember as a happy place, where you feel safe. The more you can practise this - you don't have to sit chanting - meditation can be done on a bus or the tube - the more peace and light you will be able to conjure when you need it.
And that is the key.

Learning to trust The High Priestess
Take her from your pack and look at her..

The Juggler

Now, *really* look at her.

Look at the face, the robes, the colours. You've already identified with this card in Chapter One.

She is the key to changing your life by using Tarot; she is the dance mistress who puts you in step with the Juggler.

In my (extreme!) youth there were magazines for schoolgirls called things like 'Bunty' and 'School Friend'. I was always unsure what kind of schoolgirls they were aimed at - school*gels,* I think, but they were OK. No sex, of course, since that was not invented until Mick Jagger; but they did have stories about boarding schools ('Tuckshop Trudie Saves the School') and ballet schools ('Born to Dance!') In the latter, the school was always run by a beautifully elegant, ex-ballerina who had suffered some terrible misfortune on-stage and now walked with a stick, but who could recognise Swan Lake material as Mummy's car turned into the drive. Looking back now, that was one of my first perceptions of the High Priestess.

She is your muse, your inspiration. She is the teacher you had at seven who introduced you to Terry Pratchett or Tolkien. She is the whisper in your ear at seventeen when you began to question established religion. But of course, she never demands of you, she never invades or evangelises you. She never will. As in the Tarot, she is simply an option.

Life - like a Tarot reading itself - is a series of options. It never gives answers, and nor will she. But if you want to ask her; if you say honestly that you are on a questing road - the High Priestess will never fail you.

In learning to trust her, you are actually learning to trust yourself; your intuition, your 'gut feeling' . But it helps to have a focus - after thirty years reading the Tarot I still need

The High Priestess

the image of my High Priestess before a client arrives, and also for every magical working I do in the name of the Goddess and her Lord.

I don't always have her *physical* image in front of me, but my own depiction of her is burned into my brain, almost, and it becomes automatic to call on her. Start to try to do this too. You like your Tarot pack's image of her - or you would not have bought your deck.

When you begin a reading, or go into your workspace; when you meditate to quiet music or simply when you're stressed out and don't know what to do - try to see your High Priestess. Picture her between the backs of your eyes, at the top of the back of your nose, inside your head.

It doesn't matter if you are male or female, by the way - she is the most important card in your pack.

Some of us simply call the Goddess (whom the High Priestess serves) the Lady. Other names for her are Aradia, Habondia, Ishtar, Diana, Isis, Freya, Cerridwen - all are names by which the Lady is known to us. She is personified by the Triple Goddess - the Moon - triple because she has three aspects, the Maid (New Moon) the Mother (Full Moon) and the rather - to our modern ears - 'ageist' Crone (Dark of the Moon). We will look more at the significance of the Moon later, when we explore her Tarot card.

Magic, of any kind, is not a light thing. In calling on the Juggler and the High Priestess you are in fact calling on deities far, far older than Christianity.

Gentle Ritual to Begin a Slow Waltz
Go into your special place, taking with you the items listed at the beginning of this chapter. The idea of the tray is so that

you can check you have everything to hand before you begin. It destroys atmosphere if you have to leap up to fetch something in the middle of your ritual, and if you follow this course and begin circlecasting you should not break the circle, no matter what you've forgotten. So, get into the habit of putting items on a tray which you can carry in with you, having checked it first.

The flower or fruit should be as local as possible - from your garden is obviously ideal .

You are going to drink the water or wine, so it should be palatable! Try to find a pleasing glass for it - under no circumstances should plastic ever come into contact with your natural magic vessels!

The joss stick should be a smell you like, obviously. For the beginner, sandalwood is gentle, mind-expanding and sweet. Frankincense and myrrh are actually wonderful for natural magic, and you can buy them in joss form. For real incense you will need an incense burner. Don't worry about that at this stage. A sweet smelling joss or a couple of drops in an oil burner, if you have one, is perfect.

The white candle is your centre candle, representing Spirit; light, love, Ether - the central white candle represents all these things. It is the flame of protection - nothing harmful can ever penetrate pure light.

The red candle represents fire, and will be used for your South corner.

You have worked out the alignment of your special place - from now on we'll call it your workplace - and you know where North is. Put all the bits and pieces on the tray in front of you, and sit down facing North..

Now; to your left is West, the Water corner. Put your glass of water or wine on your left side. To your right is East, the quarter for Air. Light your joss stick and place it to your right. Behind you is South, the Fire corner. Light your red candle and place it there.

Come back to facing North, the corner of Earth. Here you must place your flower or fruit.

Don't feel embarrassed, and above all, don't feel you must say anything. Nothing is going to happen to frighten you, so don't expect it, and don't be fearful.

At this point, some of you will remember Dennis Wheatley books, and misguided priests or teachers. Just remember this: Satan is a Christian invention. Such a creature has no relevance in paganism. Christianity's Satan evolved from a need to control and frighten people. Paganism has no Satanical figure because evil should not exist in the natural law of things spiritual. Are you out for evil or wicked intent? Then paganism is not for you, since the first law is that it will rebound, threefold. In other words, if you use magic to give out love; you will receive love back. And evil? Exactly the same.....

For those confused by the Horned God; in paganism, as in life, the Goddess must have her consort. Cernunnos /Herne bears the proud antlers of the forest king. He is an ancient, strong deity and one the early Christians sought to discredit as soon as they could.

Therefore we have the 'Satan' figure which sports the horns of the pagan Herne - the Hunter, with the horns of a wild stag.

Paganism. Now there's a word. Who is a pagan? Anyone who wishes to accept that they might be, basically. A pagan essentially follows the laws of nature, and worships the earth;

the turnings of the seasons, what we call the Wheel of the Year.

Now, light your white candle; the centre candle; that of Ether, and dedicate your quest, your High Priestess and yourself to the pursuit of spiritual truth. Put the white candle centrally in your workspace, light it, and speak your truth. Don't mince words. In my experience, the gods are angels are humans who've made it back again. If you want to say please, I've f***** up my life, help me, then say it. Equally, if you are feeling especially glad - and acknowledging the corners, even this simply, can have that effect, then express it. That warm feeling inside your solar plexus area is the beginning of your dance with the Juggler.

Nobody is listening except the spirits or gods you've asked into your life. So pour it out. Watch the centre candle. This is Ether, which represents Spirit. I don't need to tell you what to look for - it will happen as it needs to for you personally, and you will know that someone is hearing you.

At this point there is no circle, although we have identified the four corners. Be content to sit inside the four quarters, concentrating lightly on your Ether candle, and feeling calm.

Learning about the Juggler

Why not 'learning to trust the Juggler' too, as you must learn to trust your High Priestess?

Because you can't, and you mustn't. Dance with him, but put your faith in the dance mistress.

Why?

The Juggler also has the name 'The Magician'. He is, for all you scholars of Greek and Roman mythology, equated with

Hermes and Mercury respectively; the all seeing adept; the only one of the lesser Gods who had the bottle to defy Zeus. On the table before him, in a traditional deck, you will see that he has the symbols of the four Elements. A sword (air) a cup (water) a pentacle (earth) and a wand (fire). He has these because he controls them, and he is the supreme practitioner of natural magic. He is the conscious link between Ether (Spirit) and the Earth. He will partner you in the steps of the dance; he will smile, he will flatter, he will encourage. But in the end, he will expect that you have trained yourself to understand.

The Juggler, being male, is sometimes seen as representing the servant of the Lady's Lord; who we know now by names such as Cernunnos or Herne - or indeed, the Green Man, lord of the Wildwood.

These are not frightening concepts. The Lady and Lord are all-knowing; they are aware of the gentleness and sincerity of those who practise Earth magic. We solitaries are known as 'hedge witches', and with the aid of this book you may learn that you'd like to be one, or at least to know one as a friend, because the little rituals which will enable you to dance with the Juggler can grow into greater ones, or stay as simple as you wish. Remember, with all things magical and 'Tarotic' - it is your choice and option. Nobody else's - and *nothing* else's!

When you feel ready, pick up and look at your Juggler.

You may wonder why you aren't first studying The Fool. The reason is the meaning of The Fool, which we've touched upon. The Fool is unnumbered because he represents the beginning and the end of the Major Arcana - the beginning and end of a cyclic journey.

But The Fool is unsure. In a reading he would represent to you, the reader, that the querant was uncertain about the direction his life should be taking. The Fool at the beginning of a spread is a sign that this is why the querant is consulting you. He does not know whether he should proceed along his new route. The cards that follow will obviously tell you whether to advise him to or not.

But you *have* chosen. You are *not* unsure. You've bought this book and got this far into it. You've *decided,* and your road, although unknown to you, is not uncharted. What you need is the *confidence* to proceed, and that is what The Juggler will give you. He is a Magician. He is the great communicator; the card of study, of learning; he is the connection between you and the magic which you seek. Look up the traditional meaning of The Juggler at the back. Now look closely at your card. Identify with it. See yourself there with him. See yourself opposite him, perhaps looking at the goods he offers as you would at a market stall.

On the table, in front of him, he has the four elements; the keys to life spiritual. So do you. Your tray contains them.

Your representative at your North point - the Earth corner - is your flower or fruit; a gift of the Earth, gifted by you back to her. The Juggler has the pentacle.

He has a dagger, or sword, which is the Tarot symbol for Air. Your traditional pack will show the Ace of Swords bursting triumphantly through clouds. Your joss stick is a somewhat milder image of Air, but no less powerful for the moment.

The cup, or chalice, is instantly recognisable - Water, obviously. Your own glass of water or wine, placed in West's corner, is your homage to the element of Water.

The fourth item on your Juggler's table can, depending on your pack, look more like something the dog did on the floor than what it actually is, which of course is a wand, or more usually, a sprouting branch or cudgel. This represents Fire, and in a few helpful packs is seen to be producing flames. This is your red candle, placed in South's corner.

So, you see that you are now well on your way to understanding the symbolism of the four elements as they relate to the four corners which will eventually form your magical protective circle. You've also learned, without needing recourse to the back of the book, the elemental drive of each of the Tarot suits.

This evening, sleep with your High Priestess under your pillow. Any dreams that you remember, write down. From now on you must always have a pen and paper by your bed. Often waking/dreaming thoughts can solve many things. (Again, more later.)

Of course, there is sometimes a price to pay to The Juggler. As with any teacher, his time is precious and not given without a fee.

The Juggler asks that you learn the steps thoroughly and make sure you like the dance before he takes you on to the next level, and so it will be with you.

The Juggler can have his negative aspect - all the cards do. This is their reversed mode which is a subject for the appendix chapters. Remember for the moment that a positive attitude to *anything* will help you in life; and in earth magic, which relies heavily on the positive and negative, it is essential.

However, The Juggler reversed is worth mentioning at this stage because he will be saying *think about this carefully. Are you sure?* In other words - The reversed Juggler is *not* confident, so nor should you be. The Juggler reversed is an important card to know in terms of negative aspects.

For example, if reading for a particular project, The Juggler reversed would not bode well for its success - but the cards that follow should be carefully studied, because The Juggler is always your teacher, and it may be that he wants to show you that a different path may be better. He will then show you, if you ask him by isolating him and simply questioning his reversed image - called 'enhancing' - see appendix chapter 'Enhancing' - what you should try, or what qualities you need to import to the project for its success.

So remember that negative cards don't always mean hopelessness. I've found this to be one of the major faults of novice readers - they ask, for example, 'should I trust this lover?' and get a table full of swords. Since they actually are crazy about the person, they refuse to accept there might be any problems and immediately blame their cards, or their lack of skill or 'psychic ability'.

What they *should* do is find out what the problems are, by isolating the beloved's card, perhaps, or the worst sword, and just *asking*. If you love your cards enough, they will throw themselves about the *room* to please you. (Not yet though! Don't expect them to do it next week! It happened first to me after several years! But it *did* happen.)

You must always be positive.

You just *don't* say, 'it says in this book do this when the moon's waxing, but what if it isn't?' - do you?

Believe in your own abilities and learn to trust the spirits of the Earth. If in doubt, use your meditation and your High Priestess and just *ask*.

Chapter Four

The Festivals and Seasons

You've now read enough of this book to decide whether or not you want to go for it. At the end - I've called it the Appendix Chapters because I remember in my childhood a friend's brother had his appendix in a jar and the appendix chapters in this book are a bit like jars that one finds in forgotten larders - full of divers and strange things.

Here you will find what I call the 'sound byte' bits for the Tarot and, if you want to, you can skip all the rest of it and go straight there. But if you do, you'll be doing what the little books that come with your cardpacks tell you and it *isn't the same*.

The rest of this book is concerned with the pagan festivals at the seasons and their relevance to the Tarot. If you follow this through, you won't just be reading on autopilot.You're learning Wicca, as our American brothers and sisters love to term it, but Witchcraft is what it is, ever was, and ever will be.

Witchcraft and the Tarot
Nobody was ever burned as a witch in England - a fact that surprises some people. Suspected witches were hanged here.

In Europe - a fiercely Catholic place - they certainly were burned alive, in their hundreds. And in their hundreds they were hanged in England, which may - or not - be a more pleasant form of death but which is certainly as unjust.

The women selected were the midwives, the village seers, sometimes the emotionally inadequate; the 'loonies'. The elderly woman living alone in her cottage with a cat fared as badly as the twenty year old up the road who had bedded the squire and his wife didn't like it.

In this way, a benevolent and gentle craft which had been practised for centuries was eradicated within a generation. Anyone could be denounced as a witch, and be investigated by the Christian church, usually with disastrous results. Most people have read of the 'tests' used to 'find' witches.

(We now face a more enlightened future. With the repeal of the Witchcraft Act in 1951, paganism was liberated. And yet - I find in my own circle that an older couple - only in their sixties - still cannot come to terms with being able to be open about their lifelong faith, and many people in certain occupations (teaching, politics, local government, to name a few) are understandably secretive and sensitive about their pagan beliefs.)

What was needed during the Persecution was a secret way to communicate the knowledge, the old lore that the wise women knew. By this time there were precious little of them and their numbers were dwindling every time a witchfinder knocked on another door.

During the Persecution, covens deliberately severed connections with each other so that under torture they could not give away names.

The Tarot - although it is presumed not to have originated in Europe - was known well through its Italian decks. It became the Arcana - the book of mystical knowledge. An ARK. A keeper of the unknown. And so the Major - picture cards - evolved, and the Minor - originally for playing with, exactly as our own playing cards with the familiar four suits are. And these seemingly innocuous cards, which the wise women continued to use although under threat of persecution, have become, in the 21st century one of the most important magical aids of pagans and/or witches.

We have the choice now of hundreds of different packs. There is one out there that wants to be owned by you if you've read this far.

The point is - go back to the beginning if you're itching to use your dream pack. Look at the first chapter and the important A bit. Keep to your Morgan Greer./Rider Waite just for this year. Buy your lovely deck and keep looking at it.

Okay, we're into Natural Magic now, and you are never going to be the same again.

Ready?

The Empress

Chapter Five

Imbolc - February

Learning how to touch Earth

You will need for this chapter:

From your Tarot pack - The Empress, The Emperor and The Heirophant

A wild flower or bud, or a fruit of the season

photographs or other memories of your childhood

a glass of water or wine

a joss stick

a red candle

a white candle

notepad and pen

your High Priestess

the tray

Understanding the Empress and Emperor

I know! 'Understanding' is not the same as learning about, or trusting. No. The Empress is up front, relatively. She has none of the underlying spirituality of her sister the High Priestess, and none of her powers. She's Sharon, your next door neighbour with five kids. She's you, if you have children and are female. She's your mum.

The Tarot, with regard to the Empress and the Emperor, is not politically correct. But then it wouldn't be, would it? Is life?

The Emperor

Do we *really* want it to be? I suspect not.

Here, because we are dealing with the Earth's awakening, we are going to study in more depth the Empress and the Emperor. Yes, I know the High Priestess is number two and the Heirophant is number five, but we can't learn these cards in sequential order.

These two cards, sandwiched between the representations of male and female spirituality, are the earthly 'parents', if you like. The Corn Mother and the Oak Lord. Deities still, but that part of the Goddess and God which relates to Earth. So here is your mother, and you as mother. Here is your father, and you as the paternal aspect. In basic 'sound byte' terms, the Tarot is not politically correct at all, since the Emperor represents the head of the household, and the Empress the head of the domestic arrangements, and carer of the children. And no, in the Tarot I'm afraid it doesn't matter, Mrs Smith, that you are the Chairperson of Microsoft UK, you are still the Empress if you have children of your own. Your husband stays in bed all day eating chocolate? You have children with him? Sorry. He's still your Emperor.

These two cards are quite important to get established. *Is* the Empress yourself/your querent? If you/she are not a mother, probably not. Possibly your own mother, then, or a mother figure? Once you can look at a reading as a whole and see what it's telling you (and you will, no matter how daunting it may seem now - as long as you *practice*) you will also know whether the Empress is simply representing the other thing she does - the querant's creativity.

The same is true of the Emperor. If he represents your husband, then he is doing so as head of the family. If he is you, then, if you have children, then this is you as father figure. But he can also stand for independence - the motivation to lead with your 'masculine' side.

An interesting deviant to this rule is when there is a dispute between husband and wife and/or parents of the children. Normally, a lover/husband/wife would be represented as a King or Queen - hopefully, a matching card to the querant's own significator, which would point to the relationship being positive.

I have noticed that where an Emperor or Empress pops up in an initial reading (and all the tentative readings you may be doing now, whether they are simply drawing one card off or three, are 'initial readings') they often represent the spouse who seems antagonistic to the querant.

For example, if reading for a woman whose cards have shown distress (swords) with emotions (cups), an Emperor is likely to be the man who causes the problems, *but he will also be the father of her child/ren, or his own will be the cause of her* problems. A lover will simply be represented as one of the kings. An Emperor with the same sort of reading with a lot of pentacles will show material aspects of that relationship which should be sorted out - but little need to concentrate on the emotional side of the reading - much more the financial/property/security aspects.

So, you say, fine. How do I 'get' these cards? How do I find them from the seventy eight cards in my pack so that I can read them? Flip to the appendix and 'Finding the Cards'. You still have to play. All the time you are looking at your cards, usually in frustration at this stage, you are learning. Remember that your High Priestess is your key. She is the one card you must always keep in your mind. Try conjuring her image in quiet moments everywhere - on a bus, in a boring lesson, in the bath. Fix her solidly between your eyes, and the rest of Tarot will follow her.

The Heirophant

The Heirophant, also known as the High Priest, is the consort of your High Priestess. He is also the representative of your querant's spirituality. Because in my method of teaching Tarot the High Priestess is so essentially yours, we take the Heirophant to illustrate his or her own higher self.

I often use the phrase, when The Heirophant is present in a reading - 'send it upstairs' - a phrase I've used elsewhere in this book! I then ask the querant if he/she understands what I mean. Some people will grasp it immediately. Others will need an explanation. But where the Heirophant is present you almost always have someone who is spiritually aware in some way. But he is spirituality as they perceive it - if they are Christian, he will be God. Muslims will see him as Allah. People with alternative beliefs will choose to see their Heirophants as; perhaps, their own higher consciousness; their guardian angel - whatever. It's important that they understand that The Heirophant is *their* spiritual guide - whatever their personal faith or religion. Never impose your beliefs on others, and remember that The Heirophant is to your querant what The High Priestess is to you.

Imbolc is:

2nd February
The 'white' festival for the Goddess as Maiden - Spring.
Christianised as Candlemas
Sacred to Bridget, or Bride, Christianised as St Bride
The festival to bless the land with the seed of the Sun
The time when the young Sun God (born at Yule Solstice) pursues the Maiden Goddess and impregnates her with what will, at Lammas, become the harvest.
A time of cleansing, purification and new beginnings.

The Imbolc tree is the ash.
The Imbolc flower is the snowdrop.

The Hierophant

46

Bride

Bride, Bridie or Bridget, is a pagan goddess especially associated with wells and springs. At Imbolc, she represents the Goddess as Maiden - Spring. Her flower is that of the virgin - the snowdrop. She is also the Lady as New Moon, the young moon with her fecundity burgeoning with the spring. She is visited at Imbolc by the Sun God, who was born at Yule, and who has grown remarkably fast to virile youthful manhood. (Gods tend to do this.)

I once attended a memorial service at St Bride's Church, Fleet Street, which is the journalists' church, where the vigil for John McCarthy was held during the years he was held a hostage in Beirut My husband is an ex-Fleet Street journalist and the departed was a colleague. As most people know, there is a River Fleet, which still flows into the Thames, culverted beneath what is now Fleet Street. St Bride's church is sited over one of its springs. It would originally have been a pagan shrine to Bridie.

Inside the church, there are two large statues, looking over the chancel and congregation. One is St Bride herself, and the other is St Paul - another pagan-turned-good-guy on the road to Damascus - allegedly.

Traditionally, Imbolc is a 'white' festival as opposed to a 'green' one - i.e., Nature is dormant and not in full leaf.

The flower of Imbolc is the snowdrop. I live in Buckinghamshire, which is hardly Siberia, yet some years I have not been able to find a single wild snowdrop to deck my altar on February 2nd.

You don't need to celebrate Imbolc on February 2nd.

If you want to, of course you can. But earth magic is very flexible, as are the people who follow its winding course through the ever-changing hills and valleys of human perception. With all the pagan festivals, the *feeling* is all.

Go out into the woods and fields. Visit your park or gardens if you live in a city.

Look at the moon.

The Full Moon is a celebration in itself. If this coincides with your first view of a snowdrop, or the brave shoots of celandines in your local woods, then that is your Imbolc.

I will always remember a childhood visit to Burnham Beeches, near Windsor and not far from my home, with my father. I must have been about eight or nine years old. Usually, my mother came too on any family outing; but she was very ill during this period and I had been sent to stay with my aunt in Kent (for what seemed a very, very long time) while my mother was in hospital.

I never forgot the ancient trees and the burgeoning growth pushing up beneath them: it was as if the springtime I'd seen had been cut short by the trauma of my separation - not just from my family, but from the beechwoods into which I'd been born . Kent - a beautiful county - just wasn't the same as my own hills. Already I was a pagan.

Roots

You will have your own, and the feelings of belonging with a particular tree, or a mountain or hill landscape; a river perhaps - the Mersey and the Tyne being obvious examples.

The canals, which carry their own tradition and which pass through many towns whose only claim to existence is these arteries of another century's heartbeat, are surely the holiday of the questing pagan. If you don't touch Earth (without trying!) somewhere on the canal system of England, you must eat your own woolly hat, which is clearly covering your eyes and ears as well as your soul.

So speaks one born inland - the spiritual allegiance to the sea being, I think, one of the ultimate places its lovers can never leave.

Roots of being, rooted in the earth which first gave you breath, and which you never forget.

Imbolc has been Christianised as the festival of Candlemas, or the Purification of the Virgin Mary. It falls 40 days after the Winter Solstice: i.e., Christ's birth, which in ancient times was the period necessary for the cleansing of women after childbed. It is the time of rejoicing that at last winter is showing signs of being at an end. Our ancestors, who relied far more on the seasons for survival than we do, recognised Imbolc as a sign of rebirth, and here we have echoes of the Greek myth of Persephone, returning from Hades to bring the Springtime back to Athens.

The Farrars' book 'The Witch's Bible' (see bibliography) gives two wonderful suggestions for making a crown of lights, which is traditionally worn at Imbolc. One is positively Blue Peterish, with instructions on how to hide the batteries in a kind of French Foreign Legion flap at the back of ones head. This is all proper and great if you want such high tradition but it isn't the way of the hedgewitch, or natural magic. Candles on the head may lead to awful consequences in the wind in a field or a on a hill in February; and those are the places you are most likely to want to be.

Candles are traditional, of course, and the Farrars are only trying to be helpful with their hidden battery.

The crown of lights was a crown fashioned with candles and placed on the head of the maiden of the coven.

Traditionally, the Imbolc festival was observed by the women, probably *because* of the virgin aspect of the young Bride. The circle was cast using the chaps, and the candle ceremony performed, of which more later. The chaps are then basically sent off to the pub..

The ritual for Imbolc being over, and the men departed, a specially prepared wand is brought out. This wand is just for Imbolc, or adapted to be so, and has a very phallic quality about it. For instance, it could be a thinnish stem of ash with an acorn on the end, or an oak cutting with a pine cone at its tip. You get the picture.

The other requirement for the ceremony is a Bridie biddy.

A Bridie biddy is a corn dolly, made with last year's straw, and dressed, or draped with a scarf or some other fabric to resemble a woman.

Corn dolly makers - and it's wonderfully surprising how many there are - can usually be found at Craft Fairs, and your local Women's' Institute will probably be able to put you in touch with one, through their list of speakers. They will all know how to make a Bride's Cross (or, of course, *Saint* Bride's Cross!) and this is the basis for the Bridie biddy.

You dress the cross as if the four arms were a person - one for the head, the two corresponding ones for the arms, and the (one) leg being covered by the scarf, sometimes in white lace and silk and satin so that the image actually resembles a bride.

The biddy would then be placed in the ashes of the fire and a favouring spell cast to Bridie on her night. The phallic wand was placed by her side. If, in the morning, a male footprint was seen in the ashes beside the biddy (it always was, of course, since the blokes were in the pub and *someone* of their number would have remembered to put the boot in, as it were) it was advantageous for your crops and you rushed out and sprinkled the booted ash on to your fields.The virgin Bridie had been fertilised, and so had your land.

The Celtic name for Imbolc was Oimelc, meaning ewes' milk. Indeed, Imbolc is a very feminine festival, and that's why it would be a good time to dedicate your learning to Earth - whether you are male or female.

Earth energies are always feminine. The Earth is always depicted as a goddess. She renews herself as the virgin Springtime, the maiden goddess, ready to be impregnated by the rebirthed young god.

Here we have one of the main difficulties in explaining the male/female personae of earth magic. The Goddess at the Winter Solstice gave birth to the Sun God. The rejoicing at the Winter Solstice (December 21st, Christianised as Christmas) is for the return of the sun, and so the wheel of nature may turn for another thirteen moons. By Beltane (April 30th) he is a young, virile man and lays frequently with the Goddess to produce that season's crops. In other words, the understanding of natural magic is in the basic acceptance of the Goddess as the main deity, the mother/wise woman/ virgin transformation as the full, waning and waxing moon; with the God - the male personification of nature as the sun - and of the son to the mother, as well as representing her lover. Some people can accept this concept instantly ; with others it takes time, particularly if you've been brought up within the established religions.

If you can't understand the fundamental thinking behind it - don't worry - the festivals and seasons *are* it, so as you learn about them and take part in them, it will all become clear.

Although Imbolc falls at the beginning of February, I think the best time to get in touch with the Earth energies is March. Obviously - the Earth is always there and you can call on her spirit whenever you wish, but March is the time she is youthful in her quest; hopeful and alive with the prospect of the future - just like you.

All religions have a very murky past. Buddhism and paganism are not really religions in the accepted sense, since they have no god and no insistence on the worship of one deity. Faith in oneself is indeed foremost - rather an essential!

The Tarot itself has no past to speak of, except that which is made up. It is essentially a living, growing 'ark of knowledge', which as a student of both Tarot and spiritual development you can learn to adapt to your life and your times.

It has always been so - the Tarot adapts itself easily. It's people's concept of it as some sort of rigid roster of 'meanings' that confuses both it, and the unfortunate would-be reader who gives up after all those strange little booklets that come with the decks. Burn them all, I say! And play with your cards!

Get into the habit, also, of writing notes after a meditation. It need only be a few words but it focuses you in the world again after flying and is important because it grounds you. In this, of all chapters, we are going to learn about being 'earthed', or grounding. If you're intending to fly - and you will - you need an airport to come home to. Your workspace is exactly that, and the Emperor and Empress are your flightpaths. Your autopilots

Exercises in grounding

1) You are going into your workspace, and you will acknowledge the four corners by the means we have practised so far - i.e.:

Go into your workspace, with your tray of items. Sit facing North, and calm yourself. If you like, play some gentle New Age music softly in the background. Write a few thoughts down before you begin.

Now you can see yourself as The Juggler, with your magical tools before you. Visualise your Juggler card as you sit in your workspace. Feel the confidence The Juggler can supply.

At North, place your flower or fruit. At Imbolc, the snowdrop is more significant than anything, but if you can't find one, *don't* use a hothouse flower or a tulip from abroad. A sticky bud from a chestnut tree is perfect, and fruits include catkins. Always be imaginative and remember that natural magic is essentially of *your* time and *your* place.

Celebrate when *you* feel you should. She is your Goddess; He is your God.

The Buddhist tradition says - 'in Christianity, faith in God is foremost. In Buddhism, faith in oneself is foremost.'

Who would you rather trust?

Now turn to East and light your joss stick. Ask for intuitive guidance. Turn to South and light your red candle for fire, for confidence. Turn West and place your water or wine goblet there. Ask for compassion. Then turn back to North. Honour the Goddess in whatever words you wish.

You've brought in family photographs. You know enough by now to have done this fairly instinctively. If you always hated your brother/Aunt Charlotte/ your snotty nosed niece; then leave them out. Another rule!

Natural Magic is positive.

What point is there in contemplating a photograph of people whose presence gives you bad vibes? That's all dislike is.

Your brother/Aunt Charlotte may be perfectly wonderful people - saints, perhaps. The niece may have a cold, or even some desperate sinus problem which means she can't *help* her runny nose. Fine. But for the purposes here, and at this stage, it *isn't your problem.*

So: here, for this exercise in grounding, you need the people who have or had a positive influence on your life. For most people, this actually comes down to two people at the very most - usually your parents - although not always. Only you will know.

If in doubt, which card should you ask, and how?

Always the High Priestess.

How? As you would ask a friend.

Look the card in the eyes and phrase the question. Concentrate. If you've been meditating, you should find this easy. If you haven't - and we all say we don't have time every day, don't worry - use the breathing technique (in through the nose, count to five - hold for five - out through the mouth, 12345678, and repeat) for a minute or two. (see Appendix, 'Breathing Technique')

The purpose of family photographs is to use them as your 'grounding tools'. You will have heard of magical tools like wands and swords and athames (ath-ay-mays).

All tools are symbols to enable you to enter higher realms - in other words, your spiritual state, your soul, higher consciousness - it doesn't matter what you call it.

The tools themselves are not important. It's what they *represent* to you that matters. Tarot cards are simply pieces of cardboard with designs on. But what they *represent* is something personal to you which triggers a reaction in your brain which you are going to learn not to ignore.

So, the family photographs, for the purposes of this chapter, are to enable you to 'ground' - in other words, to touch base with earth again. Before we can fly, we must first be able to know how to land, and before we get too far into the processes of magic, we must know how to use our own personal airport.

Now you are using another two cards -The Empress and The Emperor- you can imagine the High Priestess - and the Heirophant, also - as your higher, spiritual selves. You can see how the Empress and the Emperor can be described as your earthly, mundane personae. That's why they guide you back, to your 'home airport'.

Always think of your Empress and Emperor as representing North; the Earth. If you remember to connect the Emperor and the Empress with your own childhood, the photographs you've brought into your workspace, your own, earthly and fallible parents, you will begin to absorb some of the deeper meanings of both these important cards, and their difference from their twins in the higher realms: the Heirophant and your dancing mistress, the High Priestess.

What to do at Imbolc

Take into your workspace your tray, and your Tarot pack.

Imbolc - early springtime - is a time for new beginnings.

The Pagan Festivals all have their own reasons for being - the great French phrase, raisons d'etre - sums up the festivals so well. What you can do this Imbolc at the start of your new life is light a white candle. Just sit, and think. This will help. Having your High Priestess with you will help even more, and asking her to be with you in your workspace will give more strength. She'll come, if you ask her.

We'll learn more about the High Priestess and the Heirophant as we go along. For the moment, concentrate on both cards. Try to commit them to memory. This is all you have to do to make their magic begin working. That, and a rite for Imbolc, if you feel ready for this leap. This is a very simple, gentle nudge to your soul into paganism.

I teach Earth, or Natural Magic, to small groups from my cottage in the Chiltern Hills. The following is an Imbolc ceremony which is not heavy, and very much intended for the beginner. You may not wish to commit yourself to the Goddess and her Consort at this stage. You may not know who they are, although you may be aware of them. You may simply wish to offer yourself as a supplicant. Ask, and you really do receive.

With all Natural Magic, there is no set way, and those of us who regard ourselves as hedgewitches spurn the old ideas of initiation by Coven Priest/Priestess and the degree system as the 'only' path through the Craft.

This is not to say it's wrong. Such beautiful tradition has a very marked place in paganism and must be revered; but it isn't for everyone.

Personally I couldn't bear the idea of having to 'group' each month or more frequently and such covens tend to be very ceremonial. Ceremony should not be confused with ritual - which is - or can be - totally of your own making. The simple rite of cleansing my Tarot cards between readings for clients could not be more basic, but the fact that it must be done, and in a certain way, makes it a ritual, and therefore special. You will devise your own.

Can I do that? I hear you cry?!

Yes, and you *must*. In fact, it will probably devise you. If you follow my guidelines (see Appendix, 'Cleansing the Cards) at some point you may find yourself questioning. What happens if I use swords first? Or the Major Arcana sits at the bottom? Try it. You will be finding your own intuitive Tarot skills and you will know when it's working for you. Remember that your cards are like trusted friends.

You need only to be truthful, aware, and sincere. If one of those qualities is missing, you should set about finding it!

The Candle Ritual
(This was done *before* the chaps repaired to the pub!)

Traditionally, the candle crown is made to be worn by the priestess or the representative of the Goddess as Maiden.

However, for a lone witch, a young coven or you as a complete novice; the candle crown is rather complicated and I prefer to suggest, rather than the precarious and dangerous practice of wearing the crown on your head, you make a tiny one from plasticine, dedicate it with sincerity, and use three birthday cake candles.

My own group did this at Imbolc to great effect. I had bought the candles, and not realised they were the sort of birthday cake candles which re-ignite having been blown out.

Great fun was had, and also, it brought somehow a thought-provoking meaning to the fact that wishes, once cast, cannot be undone. All things happen for a purpose, and my ignorance in buying these candles was possibly the gods teaching my students a vital knowledge....

The candle ritual is simple, and can be used at any festival but is particularly effective at Imbolc, since it is the candle festival.

Each of the three candles (birthday cake or bigger!) is used for a specific wish. The candle should be lit, and the wish made. The next candle follows, and so on. After the ritual, the candles should be allowed to burn down. (Hence the plasticine crowns.)

All you need to remember is the order of the wishes.

1. A wish for the planet

This wish can be for Earth as a whole, or a part of it which is in jeopardy. There are, unfortunately, plenty of those. As you light your first candle, visualise our beautiful planet, and focus your attention on it. If you wish, focus in on the area you want to single out for attention. Speak your wish, out loud. Ask respectfully and humbly that your wish be considered.

2. A wish for someone else

This can be *anyone*. A relative, a friend, a person you've never met....someone whose plight you wish to be eased. Speak your wish aloud, as you light the second candle. Feel the power of the light coursing through the ether and surrounding the chosen person with a white - or blue (the healing colour, if appropriate) brilliance.

3. A wish for yourself
Again, all you need to do is ask with respect and humility. Obviously, asking for daft things like larger breasts or a lottery win is *not* what we are talking about here....

When working with a group, some wishes may be too private to voice aloud. In these circumstances, it is quite in order to think the wish, and to say to the group - 'My wish is silent.'

To take a branch or wand from a tree:
As with all natural magic, go with how you feel. Remember to ask the tree - if the ceremony is done with love and sincerity, no tree minds giving up something of itself to aid you.

You do not have to talk openly to the tree if you feel someone else may be watching! Trees know. Touch it, embrace it if you can but if you feel embarrassed don't worry - just *think* at it. I say again - trees *know*..

Recently I had a group of students for an Imbolc 'how to' morning, prior to the actual festival. We have ash trees in the hedge beside our house and they help to fence in the horses who graze in the field next door. Frequently, the hedge is brutally cut by those mechanical things which zip about and cause traffic chaos and flying bits of tree. The ash trees in question seem to accept their fate, since they always provide wondrous straight, coppiced branches which are lovely for my students at Imbolc, and dead on time. They're chopped down by the dreaded machine at about the same time as John Barleycorn (the God at Lammas) is slaughtered, and by the time he is resurrected in his youthful and sexual glory, at

Imbolc, there too are the ash boughs, to be cut as Imbolc wands for the following year.

One student, a young woman, refused to cut her Imbolc wand. She thought it might harm the tree, which was good thinking in a way but not in keeping with the creed. The tree will know why you want its bough at this particular time of year because you will have silently told it, and the Ash, that most magical of trees, really doesn't need to be told why a group of people, fresh from the Circle, approach it with ritual athames, or very sharp scissors.

(*never* cut a tree with a blunt blade.)

I include the following as an example of what can be done within a group at the festivals. This is a working which we do within my circle. But you must feel free to adapt it - perhaps for a couple, or a larger group, or simply taking out elements to work with by yourself.

There is no '*right*' way.

The right way is how you feel yourself.

An Imbolc circleworking

The Priestess invokes Ether with athame or wand. The white candle is charged. Dish of salt/water is charged. (charging - dedicating by visualisation and a command that the item be rendered fit for use in your work for the Goddess. Sincerity and respect is more important than the actual words, which you will find will come to you. The salt (representing earth) and water are mixed, and used to sprinkle at the centre and at each quarter.)

Wand is given to *East*, who dips it into the charged water, lights yellow candle from centre. Takes it back to corner, speaks own invocation to Air spirits.

Takes wand deosil to South and returns.

South takes wand to centre, into charged water, lights red candle and makes own invocation to Fire at her corner. Takes wand deosil to West and returns.

West (blue candle - Water) and *North* (green candle - Earth) do exactly the same, until the corners are invoked and the circle is complete. North gives wand to East, which Priestess then takes back.

It's important, corners, that you say how you feel and what you wish in your own words.

Priestess completes the circle by invoking the Earth beneath and the sky above, thus making the circle a sphere; and sprinkles the quarters, taking the wand round clockwise (deosil). She would say something such as 'Hail, Guardians of the West (or East, North or South). We ask your presence here in our circle this morning/evening.'

The wishes rite. This is particularly potent at Imbolc, because of the candles.

Ist candle - for the world.
2nd candle - for someone else
3rd candle - for yourself.

A Blessing for the Earth
(Imagine your own garden or special outdoor space as you say these words)

The centre candle is passed around the circle deosil, starting with Ether in the centre and going to East.

Ether- We remember the Goddess who left us as Crone at Samhain, and is returned to us. Welcome, Lady, welcome, Spring. We remember the young Lord, born at Yule. Welcome, Lord Sun.

Air - Lady, we ask your blessing on the birds' flight from their winter exile. May you imbue us with their intuitive knowledge, to work for humanity. May the wind blow the rainclouds to water the earth for as we need the Lord Sun we must have rain.

Fire - Lady, we ask the energy of the South. Lord of the Lady, who governs this quarter, we ask for your assertiveness during this Spring. We ask that we students of the natural laws of our beloved planet may be assisted to grow in knowledge and able to be aware of your strength. Let your warmth fill us and bless our land.

Water - Lady, we ask your love and the cleansing of the negative feelings we may have towards our fellow beings. We ask that our emotional strength may be furthered by the Guardians of the West, and that the gentle rain may bless our land. .

Earth - Lady, the snowdrops have pushed their way through the cold earth. May we work with the same vigour to further our faith in you.

West then takes the libation (booze!) from her quarter around the circle deosil, starting with Ether, or the Priestess, in the centre, and then to East, South, her own quarter, and North respectively. Make eye contact, smile, and sip from the proffered cup. It's traditional for West to give, and the coveners to receive, the cup with two hands, one on the stem and one on the cup itself.

When the libation reaches North, she holds it aloft after drinking and says

'Earth Mother, Goddess and her Lord, Blessed Be, and Blessed Be your Springtime.'

All answer, Blessed Be.

Cake is passed, and discussion may be had!

After this, the circle is opened. This is done deosil again, beginning with thanks to the Guardians of the East. The wand is taken round ESWN, each corner thanking the guardians for their presence.

This is said (more or less!) thus:

'Spirit and Guardians of the - . I thank you for your presence here this morning. Take back with you that of the element of - - which remains unused from our workings. Depart with love. Blessed be. (All repeat - Blessed be) At each corner, the candle is then extinguished.

Finally, the Priestess opens the circle, and Ether extinguishes the centre candle, thanking Spirit for its presence..

Chapter Six

Ostara - Vernal Equinox

Learning how to touch Earth

You will need for this chapter:

From your Tarot pack - The Lovers, Chariot, Strength, Hermit
A wild flower or bud, or a fruit of the season
photographs, thoughts, personal items of a lover or would-be lover
a glass of water or wine
a joss stick
a red candle
a white candle
a green candle
notepad and pen
your High Priestess
the tray

Best months to begin this chapter : March/April

Ostara, The Vernal Equinox
March 21/22

We now move on into the real birth of the year - the Vernal Equinox, 21st March.

Ostara, the Vernal or Spring Equinox, is named after Eostre, an ancient German goddess. In many cultures, ancient and modern, the stories tell of a goddess returning to the earth after dark winter months spent in the underworld.

So far, in our journey into the Tarot, we've met the Fool and the confident Juggler or Magician. We have, at Imbolc, worshipped as much, or as little, at the shrine of the High Priestess - the Goddess - as we have wished. We have felt the stirrings of our own spirituality as we contemplate her consort, the Heirophant, or the Sun God to her Moon.

There are four other cards which lend themselves to study at the Vernal Equinox. They *are* sequential, so you can wipe your fevered brow.

Let us explore the Lovers and the Chariot, Fortitude and the Hermit.

Imagine now the story of our Fool. At Imbolc, he embarked on a mission of glory, just as you are. He met his mentor, his Juggler. Briefly, he danced. He learned some steps from his earthly parents . Then, thanks to the Juggler and his teaching of choreography, he meets the High Priestess and the Heirophant. His path is clearer. He can see the Major Arcana of the Tarot in terms of the High Priestess and Heirophant being the spiritual keys to unlock a door.

He must not forget Dad and Mum, or Wife/Husband/Mother/Father. So he acknowledges that between the two poles of his new-found life (the High Priestess and the Heirophant) the Empress and Emperor - whatever they mean to him - are sandwiched for ever. He will never ever be able divorce spiritual parents from earthly ones. Man is both above and below.

The Lovers

So, our Fool travels onwards. Obviously, the first thing he encounters in his young, confident life, having had advice from the Juggler and Spirit and Earth respectively, is sex, and more importantly, his own emotional feelings towards it.

The Lovers

The Lovers represents emotional choice. It is sometimes misconstrued by novice readers as simply a sexual affair - literally, lovers. It *can* be this, but the key words to remember are *emotional choice.*

Let's look again at the Fool, journeying - for instance - through the confusion of adolescence. He is leaving childhood behind, and walking out into the great world. We know he *has* to do it, but nevertheless it's one of the biggest emotional traumas most of us ever face. Perhaps it's leaving your parents for university or the security of your childhood home for your first flat, or marriage.

Equally, it could be the mother of a school-age child going back to work, or the mother whose children have fled the nest and she now goes back to her career. It could just as easily be a woman who, faced with a new love, decides to leave her husband.

It could be as simple, in, say, a daily Tarot reading, as deciding whether with limited time you should visit an elderly parent or go to watch your son's school football match. Emotional choice, always. Never associated with finances or career - *unless there is an emotional side to it.*

For example, some people love their jobs so much that their partners feel the career impinges on their life together. Here, the Lovers is a classic card, particularly if surrounded by a mixture of the four suits. Choose, it shouts! However hard it is, it's your dedication to your career or your dedication to your lover/family/bloke/girlfriend!

In these interpretations of the Major Arcana, always keep the 'journey' in mind, because it helps you with the literal translations of the cards. When the Fool is presented, *know* your Tarot story and *see* your querant at that cross-roads in his life. When the Lovers is presented, it should trigger the words 'emotional choice', but as with all intuitive Tarot reading, the trigger is just the beginning. You look at the cards around it. A King or Queen in the spread is obviously a good springboard. Who is this person? How is he or she involved with your querant's emotional choice?

Why? How? Always ask this of your High Priestess, silently, sincerely. Be aware that she will always answer you. Trust.

At this point, I want you to go to the Appendices. We are going to visit a pub!

Turn to the Appendices at the back of the book and read the Chapter called 'Tarot Street, or South/West/North/Eastenders' (I know. Terribly witty)

See you after the pub.

Queqants, Kings and Queens

Let's imagine you have a querant in front of you.

You vaguely know your characters now, from the pub, so you can decide on the nature of the man or woman concerned. Contrast him/her with what you already know about your querant, and think - if your querant is a Queen of Cups, and the Lovers is followed by a King, assess the situation. You must never tell your querants what they should do - that isn't your role. The Tarot only gives options. But imagine just two scenarios.

1. Your Queen of Cups querant is followed by the Lovers, and then the King of Swords.

2. The Queen of Cups and the Lovers are followed by the King of Cups.

Don't worry for the moment about how she, or the other two cards actually got there - significators, spreads and lays are in the appendices.

What is your gut reaction to the relationship as depicted in 1?

And what about in 2?

Don't try to use any subtlety. You don't know enough yet. Is it good or is it not? Yes or no?

Now, in both, your querant has a choice, and her choice is whether or not to get involved with the King. We know this, because the Lovers - the emotional choice card - comes between her own card, which she has chosen (again, this is in the appendices, 'Choice of Significator' ; don't worry about this now) and the King.

In 1, she may have just met, or is having to decide about a relationship with the King of Swords.

In 2, exactly the same, but with the King of Cups.

Just go with your reaction to both Kings.

You want to advise her to go with the King of Cups, don't you? But you're unhappy about the King of Swords and you're not sure what to say.

Absolutely right!

You've just assessed, intuitively, your first partnership. Well done.

Play with the other Kings and Queens, knowing what you do about them from the pub. Let your mind wander.

The Chariot

Can you match them to some of your friends and relatives?

The Chariot

Look at the card. It's a strong card in most packs. The card of battles and fights. Our hero, the Fool, having loved, has now gone for a soldier.

You, journeying through this book, have suddenly encountered a battle, haven't you? You can't see where this is all leading. You're intrigued, but all sorts of other things are clamouring to gain attention in your life and you are wondering whether it's right that you should learn the Tarot and what appears to be a smattering of white witchcraft anyway, aren't you?

Remember this - although the Chariot speaks of a fight for the Tarot querant - that's you in this instance - it's *always* a battle that he or she wins.

So, if you decide to give up, this will be the time you do it and it will be right for you. This book may stay on your shelf for ever. You might pass it on, give it to a jumble sale, a friend. You may come back to it later, and that time will be right. You may not, and that would be right too. Perhaps it isn't, as we used to say cringingly in the seventies, your bag.

What, then, if you look at the card of the Chariot and think, sod it, I've come this far, let's go for it? Ah.

Take a step backwards and pick up your Lovers card again. Remember what the Lovers means? An emotional choice, right. This is your choice. Go on if you want to. Pick up your High Priestess.

Bring her image into the front of your head - between your eyes at the top of your nose, inside your skull.

Fortitude

What do you feel she says?

If you didn't want to continue, the Chariot would have given you the perfect out. The fact that you read on meant that you were not daunted by the battle to come - all the learning! The Tarot is all about options. You've just exercised your own. I didn't do it for you. Your own High Priestess, who is *part of you* - your higher self, your goddess, your god, your soul, your angel - whatever *you* perceive the card as - spoke to you. From now on, you will learn to listen to her, since you already know just how to ask her presence. *Learn to trust her. Always be grateful for her advice, and always thank her.*

Foꞧtitude

Fortitude, often also called Strength, is confused with Justice or Temperance in some Tarot decks. The 8, 11 and 14 are reversed. It doesn't really matter. In the Morgan Greer deck, which is one which I recommend for beginners, Fortitude is the eighth card.

Fortitude. Cool it! You have the inner strength to deal with the situation, so look at it calmly. Try to be objective.

In the terms of our two story lines - the classic Tarot journey of the Fool being the first and *you* being the second story (you've sussed that now, haven't you? Not for nothing did you make the emotional choice to continue and well done - you're in the thick of the battle but on the winning side) we can look at Fortitude thus:

Fool : The strength is within our hero. He now knows he can win any battle. He must simply be aware that he possesses this underlying strength.

The Hermit

You: Similar. But your battle is, mundanely, to learn these blessed meanings, in both senses of that word. You'll do it - we know that, because you've passed the Chariot test.

But to seriously dance with the Juggler *needs* strength and fortitude. You will have to deal with people who don't understand your choice - they may even reject you - which brings us nicely to -

The Hermit

What do Hermits do? They retreat into caves and contemplate their lives, and at this point, that is exactly what you are going to have to do. The Vernal Equinox is a great time to do it, of course, since it's a burgeoning time for Nature and everything seems possible in the early spring. (Everything, of course, *is* possible at any time. It really is, if you wish it to be so. Trust!)

Remember your special sanctuary, your workspace? Have you used it much? Some of you will have gone into it a lot and found that the more you do even simple ritual work - like lighting a candle - makes you feel significantly stronger, more in control of your life and emotions.

Now is the time to really use it

The meaning of the Hermit is 'reassessment of one's life'. Imagine it as spring cleaning.

In our dual story lines:

Fool: Looks at what he has achieved so far and finds it lacking in direction. Retreats into himself and is able to reassess his life and what he wishes now to gain from it.

You: In your own journey into spiritual development you too have reached a watershed. You've made your choice, you've run the battle through - it's probably still continuing. If you decide that your spiritual roots are in paganism you may find it'll go on for ever!

Retreat quietly into your own spiritual workspace, and assess how you feel so far. Spring, at last, is here. We rejoice with the Lady and her Lord.

Exercise for the Spring Equinox

Take all the Court cards (Kings, Queens, Knights and Pages) from your Tarot pack, plus, of course, your High Priestess, *and the four Aces.* Also take the cards we have so far studied - The Fool, Juggler, Heirophant, Empress and Emperor, Lovers, Chariot, Fortitude and the Hermit.

A word about the Aces. Think of them always as presenting a new or improved situation, and remember what each of the suits represents. (The meanings of the Aces are in the appendices.) For this exercise we are going to relate them directly to their elemental meanings.

Take out the four aces and keep them separate.

For the moment, also, we are going to use the Knights to represent moving forward, and the Pages to represent communication. Again, remember the suits.

On March 20th/21st/22nd, or as near as you can arrange, light a yellow candle and place it at East in your workspace Next to it, place your Ace of Swords. As you do so, imagine East's quarter, the Air, rushing in and filling you with intuitive calm. East is the quarter of knowledge and inspiration, so you are going to *ask* for it.

Talk to East. Explain that you feel you are lacking in your understanding of your spiritual development. Imagine you are talking to a highly respected, very wise teacher, and you are telling him or her what you hope to learn, where you feel you are now, and - yes - any fears that you have. Directly relate any questions to your spiritual aspirations. This is not the time to be asking about love affairs or career prospects!

Pick up your Ace of Swords and raise it high. *Feel* the heaviness and power of the sword as it slashes through the air. *Know* that any problems cast your way may be dealt with by the glittering Sword of the East. Place the card back by your yellow candle.

(If you *should* feel a little frightened, focus on your High Priestess, or simply pick her up and ask her protection.)

Move deosil to South. Light a red candle and hold your Ace of Wands aloft. *See* the tip of your Ace of Wands surrounded by fire. Feel the power as you imagine your card as a strong, wooden shaft perhaps, or a smooth precious metal. *Know* that the magical strength of the South can help you with all opportunities. Place the card by the red candle.

Move deosil to West. Hold your Ace of Cups aloft. Imagine it heavy with wine, water or mead. Bring it down to your heart. Imagine the power of Water coursing through you, filling you with love and compassion. Place the card by your blue candle.

Move deosil to North, and your green candle. Hold your Ace of Pentacles high. Imagine it as a bright, shiny coin which turns into a breadboard. Know that by its power you will not want of earthly things. Say something of your feelings to the Lady, whose quarter this is.

Acknowledge the sky above you and the earth beneath you. Sit quietly in the centre of your circle and breath deeply a few times, letting your breath go fully as you breath out through your mouth.

What you are going to do now will effectively be your first Tarot reading guided by Earth magic. Using East - guardian of knowledge and intuition, who better? - you are going to select, first of all, what's called a *significator*, a card to represent the person who is asking advice - in this case, yourself.

If you are female, spread the four queens face up in front of you. If you are male, use the kings. You know a *little* about the qualities of each suit, but not much, which is why it's still possible for you to be able to do an exercise such as this one.

Later, you will find your own knowledge a hindrance to reading for yourself. You won't be able to be objective when you and your cards have become an item. Alternatives are to visit other readers (but you have to find one you can trust) or other ways - explained later on. Don't worry about this now. Rejoice in your new found brilliance!

Now choose a queen or king to be yourself. Do this as instinctively as you can - going with your first choice. Pick up the card, and look into the face of the queen or king. Try to imagine your own face looking back at you, as if you were looking into a mirror. (This is sometimes easier if you half-close your eyes, or if you try to look *through* the card rather than *at* it.) Place it face up to your left.

Now put the remaining queens or kings face down, and place the other cards - minus the aces - face down on top. Shuffle them, facing your East quarter. Shuffle however you like - face down on a table; conventionally in your hands - it doesn't matter. Mix them well. At this stage we are not concerned with reversed cards so don't worry about that.

You should have twenty five cards in the pack, the four aces by the candles and your significator face up to your left.

When you've shuffled or mixed your cards enough, put them face down in front of you.

Now see, between the backs of your eyes, the image of your High Priestess.

You won't be able to look at her 'in the flesh' as it were - she's somewhere in your pack of twenty five. This is where your developing powers of visualisation begin to be important. 'Imagine' her. Really *try* to remember her colours, her position, her expression.

The next process is done in one of two ways.

This is very much a learning thing and is not necessarily how one would normally read Tarot - although remember, as with everything else concerned with Natural Magic - to go with what *you* feel is right, and to reject anything you instinctively feel is wrong *for you*. Don't listen to what anyone else says you 'must' do.

Those rules apply to this little exercise. You are going to ask for three cards. There is no right or wrong way of doing this, but you will know which seems right for you. Before you start, look into your candle flame. Remember all that you asked East. Repeat any questions, if you wish.

Put your pack of twenty five cards face down in front of you. Call your High Priestess into the back of your eyes. Ask her for a number.

If you 'see' or 'hear' a number - and it *will* be between one and twenty five because your High Priestess is not stupid - count from the top of your pack and if, for example, she gave you 'seven' it's the seventh card you select. Put it face down to the right of your significator. Do the same thing twice more, so that you have three cards beside your Queen or King - the 'you' card for this reading.

Option two. Okay - you've tried the above and either a jumble of numbers came into your head and confused you totally or nothing of significance came at all. Fine. It doesn't mean you are a spiritual plonker - probably the reverse. Spread the cards out with your hands so that you have a fan shape, very roughly (have you *ever* met anyone who can fan cards out properly? No. Nor have I).

Run your left palm across the cards. Now run your right palm across. One of them *felt* better than the other, didn't it? Okay. Now use the chosen hand and hover it over the cards. You will feel a tingling - or a warmth - with certain cards. *Go with the first feelings you get. At this point, don't question.* Just pick these cards up - try to limit it to three, but don't ignore cards to which you feel drawn. You won't help yourself, however, if you go on and on, thinking your reading will be better. At this stage, the shorter and more succinct your reading, the more relevant it will be.

Look at the cards, and try to relate them to your question. You know their meanings. If you can't relate to them, make sure you write the three cards down so that you can look back on them in a month's time.

What to do at Ostara

At Ostara, basically rejoice in the spring. Sit in your workspace with your candles and enjoy this renaissance. At Beltane, we are going to start circleworking in earnest. For now, on this gentlest of equinoxes (the Autumn equinox often brings gales - a thrilling embodiment of East, but sometimes wild).

Get out as often as you can into fields, woods, rivers, mountains, hills, canals - or city parks.

Look for the new shoots, love the daffodils. Determine to plant something!

Even the greyest cities have trees. Adopt one (or two, or fifty!) and visit it. City trees need much more love and care than their country brothers and sisters. Hold the tree. If you think you'll feel embarrassed, choose a tree hidden away somewhere. This is probably what was meant to be anyway, and the tree will be really responsive.

I can't explain what it feels when you empathise with a tree better than the stories of the Avebury Beech and the Little Kingshill Beech.

Why both beech trees? Because I live in Buckinghamshire which for many years was the centre of the furniture industry *because* of the beechwoods we have. Were the trees slaughtered for this industry? Of course not. They were proud to be fashioned into beautiful furniture by craftsmen who valued and respected their beauty. More were always replanted - and still are. The beech is a very magical tree and especially so to me since it has shaped so much in my spiritual life.

At a particularly bleak period in the life of my little family, my two special women friends took me down to Avebury. The three of us had been there several times before, but this felt different. They knew the stress I was experiencing, and I had burst into tears in the car on the journey down. Nobody said anything very much.

Avebury is a special place to many people. The stone circle, of course, is magical. To me, however, much as I love the stones, it's the beech high on the ramparts that calls me.

We walked deosil (clockwise, sunwise) around the embankment. We came to the tree, under which we had often sat before, just contemplating things. Beech trees have surface-roots, and this particular beech sits atop a knoll in a quarter of the Avebury ring. Its roots are amazing; forming a wondrous cacophony of tendrils and strong arms, reaching out from the bole for as far as the canopy and beyond.

I can time this exactly because we were hungry and intending to go to the Stones restaurant (another amazing place - it makes committed meat eaters like me determined to turn vegetarian if this is what veggie food tastes like).

A and L, sensing my distress and need to be alone with the tree, left me and sat a little way away, but still under the tree's canopy and, I think, in touch with it somehow. Certainly they were in touch with me.

I wrapped my arms around what I could of its massive trunk and wept into it all our problems - which had been ongoing for six months and were threatening to destroy our happiness and - almost worse - lose the cottage and the special tree-filled garden we had been creating and loving for fourteen years.

When I was returned home, a phone call had been received at the very time that A, L and I had been sitting beneath the beech at Avebury. It solved everything. It was - I have to say, not *totally* unexpected but the *how* of it was. The problem had been sorted in a completely un-thought-of way.

I took a little opal wand I keep as my 'travelling wand', and with my joyfully bounding dog went down to 'my' wood behind my house. The sun was just setting and the air was still. Something made me enter the wood by an unusual route and as I climbed the gate I saw why. In front of me was the only beech in the wood to sit on a rise with exposed roots. The sun shone directly through it, like fire. I approached it warily, astounded by it. Even the dog crept beside me. Quietly we climbed the rise, over the tracery of its roots. When I reached the trunk I saw that at ground level a small pool of rainwater had been trapped by the roots. As I bent to it, a breeze came up and whipped through my hair. We had all four elements.

The next thing was spontaneous. I cast a circle, using my opal wand. I invoked the wind and the fiery sun, dipped my wand into the pool of water and laid it on the roots of the tree. And then I burst into tears of gratitude and awe, embracing the tree.

Since then, none of us has looked back. And that is Natural Magic. It's also what you get when you consult the Tarot. Options, answers you don't understand until they present themselves.

In my case, detailed above, I'm ashamed to say I questioned my faith. I was also taking horrible HRT at the time (yes, all you super ladies, you *can* moan at me if you want because it *doesn't* work for everyone!) and it just sent me very strange indeed. It took me nearly a year to come off it, since oestrogen is very addictive - but this isn't a book about the menopause.

Or is it? We won't look at the dark lady now. Later.

Now we are loving Springtime.

A Vernal Equinox Story

I grew up, as many of you will have done, with parents who adhered to the Christian religion. And, as possibly, with many of *your* parents, they'd never questioned it. The visit to Burnham Beeches as a child with my father and my sister is mentioned earlier in this book.

It's one of my earliest memories - I think my father had just bought our first car, and this was 'the drive'. The fact that I still remember, forty-something years later, the effect that this vast forest of ancient trees had on me at the Vernal Equinox only cements my belief that pagans are born so. I remember, quite vividly, the energy of the place.

I was raised in Bucks - in the Chiltern Hills, where I still live - so I was no stranger to beechwoods and our lovely tenacious bluebells - but there was a strength and a pulsing that morning in what is in effect the last remnants of Britain's ancient forest that I have never forgotten. Quite possibly, it shaped my life to come - I couldn't have been more than six years old. Alternatively, was I coming home to a place I'd known well in another life? How can we know? All I know is that the little girl I was suddenly felt comfortable and safe, and that trees were gentle giants.

I hadn't read *Lord of the Rings* yet - it was, of course compulsory reading to be cool in the 70's - but when I did, the Ents were like meeting old friends.

Chapter Seven

Beltane

Learning how to touch Earth

You will need for this chapter:

From your Tarot pack - The Wheel of Fortune, Justice and
The Hanged Man
A wild flower or bud, or a fruit of the season
photograph or personal property of your lover
a glass of water or wine
a joss stick
a red candle
white, yellow, blue and green candles
notepad and pen
your High Priestess
the tray

Best months to begin this chapter : April / May

Beltane

April 30th
Beltane - May Eve, is the festival for the Sun God
approaching his zenith. It's a very sexual pagan festival, when
our ancestors would sneak out into the woods and do what
comes naturally, resulting in a lot of little Beltane-children
who had surnames such as Green, Wood, Jackman,*
Robinson, Robbins, Hudd (*these come from the Robin Hood
legends).

The Wheel of Fortune

At Beltane, the Earth is pulsing with new life. It seems to be the only pagan festival not Christianised, and I think this is probably because of its highly sexual nature.

To our pagan ancestors the 1st May was of great importance. It was the first day of summer, and the long hard winter was truly over. Beltane was very much a fertility rite festival, since a woman would only now be considered approachable after childbed in March.

To ensure that the Sun Child returns at Yule, it's necessary for the Earth to be impregnated also. Hence the Maypole, which was literally driven into the Earth, and then celebrated with a circle dance. It's also traditional to light bonfires at Beltane, because the festival is dedicated to the Sun, the element of fire.

At Beltane, such a male, assertive, expansive and growing festival, we'll look at the next three Tarot trumps of the Major Arcana - The Wheel of Fortune, Justice and the Hanged Man.

The Wheel of Fortune

The Wheel of Fortune is *the* fate card of the Tarot. To work with the Tarot you have to believe in Fate - that things are predestined to happen, and that what occurs to an individual is part of a greater, pre-determined plan. If you can't accept this, you will never be able to read the Tarot, for obvious reasons.

However, the Tarot is a tool by which one can possibly change the outcome of Fate, by advising the querant of the options, and allowing him/her the luxury of choice. The Wheel represents the antithesis of this - it says, go with your fate. Don't, in this instance, try to change it Go with the flow! Let things happen as they are intended to.

Justice

Well, fine. But just who is ordering this fate? *Who* has pre-determined all this? A witch will answer immediately - the Goddess. The great lady and her consort, the God.

Gaia, Mother Earth and her son/lover/consort. The Moon and the Sun. The female and male principles personified as deities.

The High Priestess and the Heirophant.

Justice

So, the Fool - and you - have learned to trust in higher beings and understand that fate is - quite literally - on the cards. Justice - the card of balance - now talks of a need to weigh up the balance between the spirituality in one's life and that bit which has to be more mundane.

Because of my role in a pagan organisation, I meet a lot of people who have newly discovered this aspect of their spiritual lives. Recently I met the girlfriend of a particularly avid devotee, and it was quite sobering. This poor girl, who was intelligent, kind and thoughtful, and clearly in love with her man, had not discovered any special spiritual pathway - perhaps she wasn't looking! It *isn't* compulsory! - but her chap - let's call him S - had discovered the pagan way and was completely besotted by it.

'He lives, breathes and almost snorts witchcraft,' she told me. 'I feel I come a bad second place to the Goddess.'

Oh dear.

S, had he consulted the cards, would have been given a firm Justice, a bit like a footballer with a yellow card. Oi! Sort it!

The Hanged Man

Balance between the divine, spiritual, *connected to the universe* and the routine, everyday - connected to the supermarket trolley and the computer terminal is more important than anything else, perhaps, in life now.

We are able now to balance our lives between the spiritual and the temporal. We have the time, for one thing. Yes, you *can* put the washing in the machine and go into your workspace to light a red candle and think about Beltane energies!

But understanding the balance of life is not without its difficulties, as our Fool finds.

Beltane is a very fiery, masculine celebration and although I'm a solitary, I like to celebrate Beltane with a bloke. We all have aspects of the other sex within us to a greater or lesser degree, and I think that to celebrate the Sun - which is masculine - how can you not have a male to invoke the God? It's a fire festival *par excellence* - and your bonfire in the garden should be a celebration to the Sun and his glory.

The Hanged Man

So - balance in your life. My friend S was loading the scales too much with his love of the Goddess and not nearly enough with his love for his own lady. To get balance right, the overloaded pan must be emptied. You must let something go.

The Hanged Man is the card of a necessary sacrifice, for the good of the situation as a whole. Your querant may be well aware that this needs to be so, but very often it's one of those 'nudges' the Tarot does so well. Usually, after the first regret at having to leave the house/job/person/situation the querant realises how much for the best this was.

Perhaps, this Beltane, your own Hanged Man is nudging *you*. What are you being so wary of letting go? Traditional, conventional things? Such as indoctrinated, corrupt established religion?

What to do at Beltane

Before the Eve, build a bonfire. If that conjures up huge piles of potentially dangerous old tyres and bits of half a forest - think again.

My own bonfires at Beltane and during the Fire aspect of my classes are in a garden incinerator. Yes - one of the those sort of dustbin things with a little chimney. They work. British weather being what it is, especially at Beltane, you need to keep your bonfire dry. And if you prepare it beforehand, with paper and sticks and wood - just as much as you think you may need but no more - you are conserving energy. If you *do* have a garden incinerator you can also make a 'wick' which pokes out of the hole in the bottom, and which you can light at the appropriate time. (My husband, the gardener in our family, always makes my 'bonfires' for me in this way!)

No garden? Don't worry. A red candle to the Sun at Beltane, watched and meditated on with intent, is just as good. As with all magic, *intent* is the key.

Go into your workspace. You are going to invoke the corners as you now know how - lighting your candles in the appropriate colours to the quarters and working deosil - perhaps, a particularly nice fat red one for South would be appropriate.

Also, *only if you wish it* , you can make a small step to furtherance of the link to the Goddess.

During the time between Imbolc and Beltane, try to find yourself the following items. You will probably find that they find *you,* in some cases.

1. a goblet, or chalice

You will only use this goblet in your magical workings, and not for a bevvy with the neighbours. And it will not be plastic! A natural substance is obviously best, and if it has been created by, say, a local potter (or if you are a local potter) then so much the better. But, like your High Priestess, you must love it. My own chalice was actually bought by mail order. I had been using one made by my first husband (who *was* a potter!) but it was in a sad state due to its years and my search to find a replacement had been in vain until I sent for a catalogue from a shop specialising in the magical arts (oh, yes. They very much exist. See appendices). What I was actually after were pagan greetings cards, but as soon I opened the package and saw that chalices were made to order I knew why I had chosen this particular company. Guess what my chalice is? Yes. A tree.

Your own search will be just as interesting and probably just as fruitful. Look in antique shops, car boot sales even - but if you fall for an old cup, be sure to purify and charge it first, to remove negative energies. (See appendices) Here again, though, purists would disagree but if it called to you in a shop it may be because it was owned by someone before who wishes you to have it because of their loving energies on it. (If you take your High Priestess in your pocket when you go chalice-hunting, you can be quite sure she won't let you buy some lump of old tat that a serial killer used to drug his victims.)

2. a wand, or athame

The witchcraft jury is out on this one. I have always used my wand to cast the circle, but many books (and witches) will tell you that you must use your athame (black-hilted knife). Well - use your High Priestess again. Wand, or athame?

There used to be a super TV advertisement for frozen chips. A little Welsh girl is asked by her bigger sister 'What do you like best - Daddy or chips?'

Choosing which tool to use for casting your circle is a bit as bonkers. Use what you feel does the best job at the time!

My wand was commissioned for me by my husband, many years ago, which is probably why I love it so. My athame is used for its function - to cut.

You will decide in the end. See what your High Priestess presents to you first!

Light your candles and concentrate on the flame of the centre candle, Ether

See, feel the fire aspect of it.

At East, you have already asked for intuition.

Face South. Ask for the guidance of the Sun in leading you towards the positive aspects of your life. Feel, as you do so, the Sun filling you with his energy. It doesn't matter if you can't see it; you know it's there.

Walk deosil to West and take the photographs of your lover. Concentrate on them there. Ask your questions, say your requests, humbly and with respect.

Pour and drink your wine or water. Concentrate, also, on the Court card you feel your lover to be. Is she a Queen of Cups you're trying to attract? Is he a King of Pentacles whose work and ambition is taking him away from you? Think on the

94

card. It's not necessary to have it with you - although it can help - by now you should be able to call up your High Priestess and any Court card to order.

Move deosil to North. Take the photographs of your lover. Dedicate your relationship into the Lady's care and leave the photograph at Earth overnight. (Take a pen and pad to bed to record any dreams or thoughts you make have on waking - either suddenly in the night, or in that half-sleep time in the morning.)

Move deosil to East. Thank the Keepers of the Watchtowers of the East for their help in your particular intuitional quest today.

Then quietly and with reverence, uncast your circle.

Chapter Eight
Summer Solstice (Litha)

Learning how to touch Earth

You will need for this chapter:
From your Tarot pack - Death, Temperance, The Devil
A wild flower or bud, or a fruit of the season, a sunny disposition and preferably some friends! (but not essential!)
a glass of water or wine
a joss stick
a red or orange candle
white, yellow, blue and green candles
notepad and pen
your High Priestess
the tray

Best months to begin this chapter: May / June

Litha
June 21st

The Summer Solstice, also called Litha, is the festival for the Lord; the Sun at his zenith. The Lady is also there, but here she plays a supporting role, as her son/lover takes centre stage. I am essentially a solitary witch and I always conduct the festivals on my own, although I teach others the basics of natural magic *just before* each festival so that they can celebrate alone, or with others, as they wish.

The Summer Solstice is the one exception to this. This festival needs a group to celebrate joy. For anyone who has ever meditated seriously, or simply is in tune with nature by walking/cycling/horseriding alone - the 'clifftop' feeling of sheer happiness and oneness with creation that a solitary attunement with the Goddess can sometimes be - the Summer Solstice is perhaps the one time of the year to seek out like-minded friends and join hands in a circle. That's all you need to do - and see what happens. You'll probably be very surprised by the strength of the feelings within your - perhaps previously uncharted! - acquaintances.

If you like, light a yellow candle at East and proceed to cast a full circle. If you prefer, the essential candle - a red or orange one, in the centre of your group is all that's necessary.

And what of the Tarot in relation to the Solstice? Ah, well. With your friends, if you decide to ask them round to your house to talk about how you all feel - whether it's a barbecue or a quiet coffee morning (or even an abandoned coffee morning - I have known them!) you are going to encounter resistance by some people. It won't be 'global' - you're talking with your friends, after all - but there are going to be some people who are going to say, no, this is not for me. Okay, it probably isn't. *Never* proseletyse. Remember my friend S?

Death

People new to the Tarot are terrified of this card. On their first lesson, going through the Major Arcana, my students have one of the basics Tarot ethics drummed into them.

If Death comes up anywhere in a spread, tell your querent not to worry about it. It doesn't mean they're about to pop their clogs or that anyone else close to them is, but if you don't tell them that as soon as you see it they won't hear a thing you say until you've explained it. They'll be staring at the Death

Death

card covertly, and they'll be worrying. It is, after all, rather a terrifying card.

The Death card very, very rarely means death itself. In the 25 years I've been reading Tarot it has presented itself only twice when I have realised that it did, and that was because of the other cards around it. In one case my querent was quite well known and I opened a paper to find her obituary there. She had died from cancer, but since she was a lady with a medical background she must have known it was terminal when she came to see me. Did I tell her? No. The Tarot is a tool for positive energies, not bad, negative ones. . She had, in fact, come to see me for financial reasons - she chose the Queen of Pentacles as her significator (see 'Choosing a Significator' in Appendices) and it was evident from the reading that she was sorting out her material affairs - making her will.

The Death card is about complete and total change and it was no lie I told this lady. For those of us who believe in reincarnation - and most witches do - it is, after all, just that. A total change.

And that is the meaning of the Death card. Unavoidable changes. The cards around it will suggest what manner of change.

By now, Litha, if you've been reading this book and practising some of the exercises, you may feel the effects of the Death card on you. As I said at Imbolc, learning to dance with the Juggler means you're never quite the same again.

Which brings me beautifully neatly to:

Temperance
Temperance means exactly what it says. Cool it. My friend S, in his mythical reading, would probably have got Justice

Temperance

followed by Temperance. Something is being done to excess. The obvious things present themselves - worrying, working too hard, doing drugs, drinking - but in fact usually Temperance is a lot more subtle. The sound byte is 'cool it' - and that's probably all you need to know. The other cards around it will suggest why or what.

Temperance in relation to dancing with the Juggler is also interesting. It's about this stage in learning Tarot and Natural Magic that students begin, literally, to take their first tentative steps on the dance floor and having 'found their feet' they whizz about, loving the steps and the music and realising what a brilliant partner the Juggler can be as they slowly change into their own High Priestess; all twinkling toes and knowing eyes.

I know - it's great. But - Temperance. Remember S.

This is the time I ask my students about their shopping habits. Are they Tesco babes or Sainsbury addicts? Not surprisingly they look at me with fear in their eyes. *This woman really is mad. What am I doing here?*

Dance with the Juggler by all means, but keep your feet on the ground. Don't *fly* with him, whatever temptation he offers - bringing us nicely to ~

The Devil

The Devil is the card of temptation. At this stage in your development, it's very tempting to throw yourself into all things magical and new age and wondrous. The Devil also cunningly offers options, one of which is far easier to take than the others. The Devil doesn't *counsel* against taking the easy way out, but he *does* say, 'Hey, babe (shrugging his leather-jacketed shoulders) this way's cooler. You don't have to put yourself through all that stuff ....'

The Devil

You probably *do* need to put yourself through all the stuff. It just isn't easy, and oh! the temptation to give in!

Your Summer Solstice represents all you've learned about your spiritual growth and its possibilities. From now on, the sun will be waning. Hang on to his strength, and don't be tempted to question the knowledge you've already gained. If you like it, go for it. If you don't, you probably wouldn't have got this far into this book!.

Perhaps others will challenge you? Be ready to meet their challenge.

Chapter Nine

Lammas/Lughnasadh

The Harvest - seeing some results from your efforts!

You will need for this chapter:

the magical tools you've collected so far (chalice, wand, athame, pentacle or coin - or their Tarot eqivalent Aces)
from your Tarot pack - The Tower (Lammas) The Star (Mabon)
a grass seedhead or ear of corn or barley
water or wine
a joss stick
notepad and pen
red, blue, green, yellow and white candles
your High Priestess
a biscuit, cake or piece of bread (home made if possible!)

Best months to begin this chapter : July / August

Lammas
1/2 August

Lammas - the pagan harvest festival - is 1st-2nd August. It was Christianised as Harvest Festival, and is sacred to Lugh, the Sun, who has ripened the crops. Hence its Irish name, Lughnasad. (*Loo-nah-sa*)

Here we have the sacrifice of John Barleycorn, the soul of the corn. He dies to provide our bread. There is a solemn rite enacted in mixed circles by the oldest and youngest male coveners in which John Barleycorn is slain by the young seed, who will provide a fresh harvest next year, and, in his turn, be slain.

At Lammas we thank the Earth for her bounty. The word Lammas comes from the Anglo-Saxon 'loaf-mass' - giving thanks for bread.

'Let us dwell on the bounty of the Goddess.

Let us think on the strength of the Lord.'

The tree sacred to Lammas is the hazel, ruled by Mercury. Hazel is the water diviner's tree, and useful for impromptu wands when needed!

The Lammas plant is barley, and its flower is the poppy.

It seems an appropriate time to harvest your own knowledge with a reading for yourself. You have six more Major Arcana cards to learn about in depth, but at this point, you're allowed to skip chapters and leap to the appendices and check on the sound byte readings of these, and those of the minor arcana, which are very much a back up, or enhancement of their bigger brothers and sisters and will provide more in-depth analyisis. (See appendices - 'Enhancing'.)

To harvest the knowledge you've gained you're going to simply ask your High Priestess for insight. There may be a particular problem or query in your life. Okay - focus on it, *as much as you can.* This means that on the day you decide to do your reading, concentrate as much as you can on the problem or query. Before sitting down to actually *do* the reading, mull over the situation.

Gather together any objects pertinent - for example, in an emotional crisis photographs are useful, as are rings/keys/items of clothing/ unwashed glasses used by the loved one/ unwashed handkerchiefs (magic can be wonderfully unpleasant). In a situation where finance is crucial, a bank statement, a coin, even a yellow flower can be the focus of your intent - because that is what it is. You are going to *think* your problem onto the cards via objects which represent it, and then ask your High Priestess, as you are shuffling your cards, to show you guidance. Remember! The Tarot never promises answers!

Go into your workspace, or to the place you find it easier to work with your cards. These are often different- they are for me. The cards obviously need a table, but your workspace could simply be a shelf/altar. If you've found this works for you too, then this is when you are going to use your Tarot place rather than your magic place.

First, select a significator to be yourself. You know enough about the kings and queens now to align one to a query you have. To ask deeper, spiritually based questions, choose as your significator your High Priestess, but remember that *nobody but yourself can ever use her as significator.* Place your significator at the left hand side of what will become your reading.

You may like to tape the following, and play it back when you are ready to begin your reading.

Sit quietly. Take off your shoes, and put your feet flat on the ground. Breathe deeply - in through the nose - one, two, three four, five, six seven, eight. Hold your breath gently, easily - one, two, three, four. Now let your breath out slowly through your mouth, blow softly - one, two, three, four, five, six, seven, eight.

106

Pull up the earth's energy through your feet. Feel it pulsing into your body, through your solar plexus, out to your hands, radiating up to your head and up through the crown to spill, like a silver fountain, back onto the earth. Then recycle it, again and again. Don't cross your arms or legs. Breathe deeply and calmly.

Become aware of your High Priestess. See her image behind your eyes. Speak to her, if you like. Address her as a friend, because that is what she is. You know she is the Goddess too, but the Great Lady is as approachable as a friend because she *is* you. She is all of us, and her Lord is the Sun to our Moon. We are, each of us, female and male.

Be aware now of her and concentrate on her image behind your eyes as you meditate on your question. Ask it - in your head - in the most simplistic way you can.

Now take up your Tarot pack and begin to shuffle. Do this slowly, *imagining* as well as feeling how the cards are mixing, dividing and falling into a pattern pre-judged by forces stronger than yourself.

Keep the image of your High Priestess behind your eyes. There will be a point at which you will want to stop shuffling. You will know it by a 'change of atmosphere', or a 'singing sound' a 'woosh that suddenly stops' - all these have been described to me by my students over the years and many more. The point with reading Tarot intuitively is that you must go with your own 'flow'. (Yuk, I know, but how else do you say it?)

Now you put your shuffled pack neatly in front of you. I ask querants to cut thrice with their left hands - but Tarot reading at this stage is about your own personal guardianship of it. If you fancy it, do it. If your High Priestess tells you to, go with her.

Now call down your High Priestess, ask her for numbers - and go.

I've taught many students to read the Tarot. Every one of them, of course, is different, and there lies a homily on reading the Tarot - bring to it your own truths/specialities/ beliefs, because that way lies the reason behind the forty-year old cry since Tarot was popularised during the sixties - *it says in my book*.......ooooooh! (For that lot of vowels read an extremely rude word - yes, more extremely rude even than *that!)*

Tarot and its arcanas - its secrets- is not about what little books tell you. It's about what you *learn* while using it. I've tried to make the learning fun in this book but there's no substitute for slog, as in every other way of life in which you aspire to succeed. You have to play, read, ask, and above all, *love* - humbly, simply, without hype or ego, and you have to learn, very gradually, how living magically can affect your life more drastically than you ever thought possible.

A lot of this is quite easily done on your own. Nobody needs a coven to encounter the Goddess. All you need is a tree. Or a seed in a glass that you can watch growing.

At harvest, John Barleycorn dies. There is a certain inevitability about this time of year. The corn is cut. The harvest is gathered. We are sure we know what is happening because it's what always happens - harvest, of all festivals, is surefire, yesindeedy as our American pagan cousins write so adorably in one of my letters from across the pond.

And so we sit back, don't we, in times of plenty, and we think, I've done it.

I've got the job/made the money/birthed or fathered the incredible baby/met my love. It all seems pre-destined until -

The Tower

I call the Tower the 'oh shit' card. My students remember it above all others - they would, wouldn't they - and this rude description implants The Tower indelibly on the brain of Tarot aspirants - they never forget it.

The Tower, like the harvest at Lammas, is an inevitability.

Look at your Tower. Lightning strikes it, figures fall from it. Do you think they knew this was going to happen? Do you think they *knew* this was 'on the cards'? No.

John Barleycorn bows his glittering golden head to the inevitable, but he didn't know it was going to happen when he surged up as a fertilised seed between Beltane's sexual energies and Lammas.

Think about what John Barleycorn represents. He is the wheel of the year, personified.

He is the culmination, the attainment, the dream. And yet his Tarot card talks of the uncertainty of life; the happenings which shatter our hopes. Imagine a field of corn, waving proudly in the breeze in one of my beloved Chiltern valleys, or the beautiful and serene places where *you* live. John Barleycorn displays himself in his glory, and then the combine harvester curls around the corner. A necessary Tower, this. For John Barleycorn, certainly. For the rest of us, bread!

What to do at Lammas

Cast your circle. Place your grass or corn, and your biscuit or cake at North, and dedicate it to the Lady. Give thanks for the food and material wealth you have. If you *don't* have it, now is the time to ask that by next Lammas your circumstances will have changed for the better.

The Tower

When your circle is cast, walk round it deosil with your wine/water and sip at each quarter. Do the same with your piece of food and, at each quarter, nibble and ingest a small piece of it. Visualise the ways in which you would like your life to change. If you have no job, visualise yourself doing what you were trained for or would like to do, and visualise your own bank statements growing. It sounds very unspiritual, but believe me, it works, and the Goddess does realise you have to live!

At the end, close your circle by the normal method. Feel positive!

Mabon
Autumn Equinox
23rd September

If you like wine, prepare to imbibe it. Mabon - the grape harvest - was sacred to Dionysus in Greece and Bacchus in Rome - both Gods of wine. We don't make much wine commercially in Britain but the tradition of home winemaking from the Lady's fruits is an ancient one. Before the arrival of the breathalyser in the 1970's winemaking clubs flourished. My parents organised one - it was held in a hall six miles from where we lived and they would always drive. It seems impossible and totally irresponsible now, but there was less traffic and people just did drink and drive.

My parents made wine from *anything*. Elderflowers, elderberries, blackberries, plums, carrots, parsley. Apples, birch sap, dandelions and rosehips. Beer from nettles. Things glugged and popped quietly in our house throughout my childhood and teens, culminating in crystal clear liquid which, when my parents were away and during my Art School days, my friends and I would drink from the fermenting jars and top up with water afterwards

The Star

The Star

The Mabon Tarot card is The Star, which is the card of dreams, hopes and wishes. It is one of the most positive cards in the deck. You will recognise your dreams. It may not be now, but you have put into process the enablement of your wish, whether or not you know it. The Star is the wish card. Its presence in a spread is very fortuitous - what you wish will come about.

What to do at Mabon

Go into your workspace. Cast the circle if you wish. Formulate in your mind a question relating to something you would like to attain - a goal, an ambition - any kind of wish. Mabon and the Wish card are also useful for other people - in this case, take a suitable significator and name it for the person whose wish you would like to aid. Concentrate on your High Priestess, and then on the Star.

Breathe your wish onto the Star. See it taking place. See it as a tangible thing - you are at that place of work/university/film studio/publishers! Be aware, through your High Priestess, that if the wish is for your greater good, it will be granted.

Now. Having come this far, I'm sure none of you are going to wish to win the lottery. The wish is a dearest held belief, perhaps something you are already working towards. You can't just wish, and sit back and wait.

What do you think this book is about? Magic?

Chapter Ten

Samhain

A Requiem and a New Year

You will need for this chapter:
From your Tarot pack - The Moon, The Sun, Judgement
The rest of your pack
Minor Arcana meanings (Appendices)
a glass of water or wine
a joss stick
a white candle
notepad and pen
a pomegranate or an apple
your High Priestess
the tray

Best months to begin this chapter : October/November

Samhain is: 31st October ('Hallowe'en') Irish Gaelic for the month of November. The pagan new year. The time when 'the veil between the worlds is thin'.

Christianised as All Hallows Eve. Sacred to those who have gone before into the Summerland.Witchcraft embraces the concept of re-incarnation, and that souls, upon death, rest in Summerland (a romantic title, perhaps, but a kind of 'working' one, since none of us can remember it, and no worse, certainly, than 'heaven'!)

The festival to reflect on the past year; remember those who are no longer with us by the observance of the 'empty chair' -

114

those who have died are never, ever called up. Witches believe it would be a dreadful thing to do this, since once a soul has left us, its progress is up to itself. But we can *remember* them at Samhain, by laying an extra place at table or acknowledging their place within a circle. If they wish to, the souls will send perhaps a flash of memory, a thought,a fleeting thought or *perhaps* a gentle touch on your arm. But to disturb them, we believe, is wrong.

A time for scrying. So you are going to use your Tarot! (Associated with the Death card in the Tarot - total change. The Samhain tree is the Elder (associated with the Crone - third face of the Goddess)

Samhain herbs are thyme (for the departed souls) rosemary (for remembrance) and rue (for the cleansing of the soul and repentance) Samhain is what the rest of the world call Hallowe'en. If you've come this far, you'll know what the 'rest of the world' is.

The festival of Samhain (Sow-in) is the only festival for which the Pagan Federation produces literature for schools. Paganism being, of course, a faith which will never proselytise, this tells you something about the concern felt by the Federation for the way some schools handled Hallowe'en. Some schools, mostly under pressure from parents who held fundamental views, ceased to hold the 'fun' parties with dressing up and bobbing apples during the eighties and early nineties. My own son, who attended a Church of England combined school because that was the village school and we had no choice, experienced severe pressure to attend church services. When I visited the school to explain that I was pagan and therefore my son should please be left alone to make up his own mind in the future, I was treated as a Satanist, which naturally, I suppose, is how they viewed me, since I wasn't one of them.

There is no harm in Hallowe'en parties with ghosts and ghoulies and warty witches all cavorting about with pumpkins! Indeed, my own group held a Samhain party in the pub which hosted our moots and I deliberated about going as Pope Joan (heavily pregnant, of course, so that I could 'give birth' on the step leading up to the pub doorway - for those who don't know the 'true'(?) story it is worth reading!) or a nun. In the end I wore the same black dress, a false nose, a wart and backcombed hair (which took me ages to get back into condition.)

We *never* call up spirits. The souls of those who have left us for the Summerland are invited back at Samhain, but only come if they wish to; and this does not mean that dead Uncle Arthur glides in through the kitchen door and insinuates his ectoplasm all over your workspace, knocking over your chalice and upsetting all the candles. He may have done this at dinner parties constantly in life, but rest assured he won't do it now.

If you go calmly into your workspace at Samhain and either cast a circle, or simply light a candle, you will not be frightened out of your wits by some white sheeted thing or a skeleton flying in at you. It's far more likely that, as you sit there quietly, a forgotten memory of a departed loved one may return, or you may 'hear' one of their favourite sayings - jokes, very often - *something* will come and you will know that at this time, when the 'veil between the worlds is thin' they return just to let you know that they live on in that place pagans call Summerland, before the inevitable reincarnation upon this earth.

The pomegranate and apple are also special at this time. Cut them in half crossways and you will see the five-fold star or pentagram. Offer this, if you wish, to your High Priestess at Samhain. Behold the fruit of death, which is life! Behold the five fold star of rebirth!

You are well enough versed in the Tarot now to know to which this kind of 'death' refers. At Samhain, all changes are possible, and within the grasp of those who ask humbly and with love.

The cards for this time are three - The Moon, The Sun and Judgement. This only leaves The World, which was my intention. The World will be studied in greater depth at Yule, but for the moment all you need to know is that it represents the ending of one cycle of your life and the beginning of another. In other words, you have studied the Tarot, and a little bit else besides. Now you can begin to truly dance with the Juggler. It is a dance which accepts the highs and lows of life as being meant; a learning process towards an absolute knowledge that there is something which guides our lives, that 'coincidences' *don't* just happen, and that what we give out to the world is what we get back. Threefold.

This is why, when people with big eyes ask me 'Are you a white witch?' It's a simple reply.

I am just a witch. Whatever you give out - 'black' or 'white' - returns on you threefold. I would rather not have a rival's spot before an important party return as terminal acne on my face. That, of course, is making light of the Law of Threefold Return.

It may not be in this incarnation, but Nature, the Goddess, the Light, or the Lady, Spirit - whatever you like - is basically good. We are all born perfect. We are subject then to things in our immediate environment which change us - our parents, schooling, siblings, relationships.

There are no 'white witches' and there are no 'black witches'. There are trustworthy people and suspect ones. And Satanists, as I've said before, belong to the Christian Devil, and he's *their* problem.

The Moon

The Moon

The Moon is one of the special cards of the Major Arcana when dealing with things spiritual - and at Samhain, we are.

The Moon is feminine, and she governs intuition. This is not to say that if you're a bloke you can't relate to the Moon - you can indeed, and if she's popped up in your reading it may be that you need to concentrate a little more on the 'feminine' aspects of yourself - spirituality, love, emotions.

Most traditional packs show the Moon as full, with her animal helpers. The Moon in a reading will show intuition on the part of the querant (not you, as the reader) and that they should use it more fully, exploring situations or solutions which may have come intuitively - or in their dreams.

The Sun

As in all Tarot pairings, we have male and female; the fundamentals of the universe. Here, we see the Sun - the masculine principle, following the Moon - the feminine, exactly as the Emperor and Heirophant follow their female counterparts earlier in the Major Arcana.

The Sun stands for assertion, for growth and prosperity. In a reading for a woman with predominantly emotional cards, the Sun will be telling her to use her 'masculine' strengths - assertiveness and possibly aggression. In a reading for either sex in a career reading it is very conducive to the growth in this part of the querant's life.

The Sun in a Wand or Pentacle based reading is growth from possibly new beginnings after a major change in work life. With the Ace of Wands, the Sun would point to a new opportunity which will lead the Querant to new heights in growth in his career and/or studies.

The Sun

The Ace of Pentacles in such a reading would indicate more security, more money or financial awareness coming from a new opportunity in this area.

The Sun is also associated with the element of Fire, promising courage. As well as embodying the male principle in a reading, he complements the Moon, exactly as, in a ritual circle, Fire (South) directly complements Earth (North).

Judgement

The 'getting better' card. The lesson of Samhain is that of rebirth - the Old Year closes, the New Year begins. And so it is with life. You can always 'rebirth' yourself into a newer, more joyous and positive future but, as I explained at the beginning of this book, you have to know how, or somebody has to show you the way.

Judgement tells us of a positive, glowing future - or simply healing. Everything gets better from that moment - the rest of the reading will have determined what the problem is, or was. 'Getting better' has obvious connotations with health, but more often it is simply the situation. The Tarot of the Old Path has Judgement as 'Karma' - which is very much an aspect of it. Judgement says, 'yes, things can improve - do you deserve for them to?' (In all probability you do, of course, or Judgement would not be in the spread!)

What to do at Samhain

I am finishing this chapter quite soon after Samhain. My little group came round the week before, as usual for all the festivals, and each had their own thoughts of those no longer with us. My thoughts were a bit more poignant, however, because we had, in fact, lost one of the group. A very gentle, truly pagan man had died during the summer at the tragic age of 36. J had helped me in my work for the Pagan

Judgement

Federation, and had discovered his spirituality helped his quite crippling disabilities.

We observed the Samhain custom of 'the empty chair'. A chair is placed within the circle for any soul who would like to sit in it. Everyone, of course, will imagine the empty chair being filled by someone they are privately thinking about.

In this case, the Samhain workshop was being held during the morning, so it was daylight. In one his first rituals with us, I remembered that J had been responsible for the Air quarter. The others had been rushing around my garden, picking a red flower here and decanting a jug of pondwater there with which to decorate their quarters. I looked up - we work from my conservatory - and saw J standing motionless underneath the dovecote, staring at the ground.

Knowing he was not very well, I was concerned and went out to him. He grinned at my query. 'I'm fine,' he said. 'But I want to decorate the Air quarter with a white feather. They'll drop one down in a minute.'

Sure enough, they did.

J was a poet and I read one of his works at his funeral. Then, instead of flowers, I laid a bunch of dove feathers by his ashes.

As I contemplated this, and the empty chair, a dove swooped down onto the glass roof above us, and looked into my eyes.

So, at Samhain, go into your space and remember those who have passed on with affection - and humour. Put out your own 'empty chair' if you like.

Samhain is very much associated with scrying, so now is the time to do your first, full reading for yourself. Refer to the appendices at the back of this book for the choice of

Significator (although Samhain is perfect for using your High Priestess as your Significator), Minors, enhancing, etc.

The 'CCT' method of card selection isn't compulsory! The Celtic Cross spread is useful for those who prefer a more constructed reading - but I do find it restricts the intuition. However, if you want to use a spread - and there are hundreds - almost every book on the Tarot (except this one) details some.

Other scrying methods you may like to try at Samhain are crystal and water-gazing, pendulum dowsing - any divination method you feel interests you but not - ever, please - a ouija board.

When you have finished your contemplation and divination, open your circle - if you have cast one - and thank the Lady and Lord, this night of all nights, for their presence in your life. Remember that Samhain was/is regarded as the pagan New Year. According to what your divination has given you; think what next year may hold.

And can't you just - already - hear the music? Can you see the glitterball and the soft lights? What are on your feet? You don't dance with the Juggler in trainers. You'll have elegant heels or soft, shining dance shoes. Or, most perfect of all, of course, your feet will be bare, to best feel the dew on the grass.

Chapter Eleven

Yule

The Rebirth of the Sun

You will need for this chapter:
From your Tarot pack - The World
The rest of your pack
Minor Arcana meanings - Appendices
a glass of water or wine
a joss stick
a yellow candle
notepad and pen
your High Priestess
the tray

Yule

Yule is : 21st December

The Winter Solstice, the longest night of the year. Christianised as Christmas. Sacred to The Goddess, who gives birth to the young Sun God. The festival to rejoice in the Sun's rebirth. The significance of candles and fires at Yule has roots in 'sympathy magic', to tempt the Sun back.

The Yule tree is the oak. The Oak King now fights the Holly Lord again, as at Midsummer, and is victorious. The Holly Lord is 'Lord of the Waning Year'; the Oak King becomes 'King of the Waxing Year'. This rivalry is echoed in the birds - the Wren and the Robin. The legend is that the robin kills the wren (little lord of the waxing year) at Midsummer, but tolerates his eggs and growth by his bounty at Yule. I'm no

125

The World

ornithologist, but I can't quite see how this adds up. However, since many pagan legends are echoed in folk song, we surely have here the basis of 'Who Killed Cock Robin?' - was the sparrow avenging the death of the wren? We shall never know!

The altar is decorated with mistletoe and holly.

The World

So - our year is complete. The World represents completion, the cycle of life's destiny closing, to allow a new phase to begin. In a reading, the World speaks about the inevitablity of a chapter of life's completion - and who knows what could be around the corner? You have completed this book. It may not have actually taken you a year but next year is to come and you may find that, once opened to conversations and meditations with your High Priestess, all sorts of things suddenly seem possible. People will 'find' you. You will 'find' people. All the time you will begin to say - 'What a co-incidence!'

After a short time, you will stop saying that, and use the term I have been using since I realised it was, indeed, true.There's no such thing as co-incidence.Having completed your cycle, you are ready for the next - you are once again the Fool, embarking on a new journey.

I have described below my group's last Yule circleworking. This is really for your interest, rather than a pattern to be followed. We have evolved over some years now and this works for us. Most of our festivals follow this basic pattern, although of course we slant it towards the energy of the festival itself.

Such a ritual circle is essentially flexible. Gardenerian and Alexandrian friends may disagree, but I am a solitary hedgewitch, using the inspiration of the Lady and Lord to set the 'flavour' of the ritual. Note that I use the word 'group' rather than coven - I'm solitary, so I work alone at the festivals. Our group meets just before, to work the circle and - if you like - rehearse what we individually feel we will do - alone usually - on the festival itself.

Our Yule Circleworking

The Priestess invokes Ether. The white candle is charged. *Ether* lights the candle and calls upon the Goddess to be with us, in his/her own words.

The Priestess charges dish of salt/water.

The wand is given to East, who dips its crystal tip into the charged water, and lights yellow candle from the centre. Takes it back to corner and speaks own invocation to Air spirits. Takes wand ceremonially deosil to South and returns.

South takes wand to centre, dips, lights red candle and makes own invocation to Fire at the quarter. Takes wand deosil to West and returns.

West and *North* do exactly the same, until all four corners and Ether is invoked and the circle is complete. *North* takes the wand to East, completing circle. When he/she hands the wand to East he/she states 'The circle is complete'

East now hands the wand to *The Priestess,* with the words 'I who have died am alive again today. So speaks East, in whose quarter the Sun rises.'

The Priestess completes the Circle and speaks.

Group breathing into - raising power. (This is simply a form of meditation together. In our group we hold hands, (and no, *not* in a certain way, you purists out there! We just hold hands. Am I a non-conformist witch? Probably) Gradually, breathing in harmony *(in* for eight, hold four, *out* for eight) we raise our arms high. We send the energies around the circle by *pushing* it deosil - from our left and receiving it with our right. Start in the solar plexus area - if it feels more comfortable, begin by lifting your arms to that level - and feel the energy and warmth and unity with your friends 'See' the cone of this group energy rising and rising. When you can see the tip of it, the apex, disseminate it onto the planet. You will usually find, with a group who have worked together for a while, that a 'group' feel develops.

Perhaps, for example, an earthquake has occurred. Without prompting, you may find a majority of your group have 'thought onto' this area.

The most common place my group send their energies to in a circle is the planet Earth herself. After all, she is our inspiration, and she needs help desperately to prevent us - humankind - from destroying her. By sending the energies up into a cone, working in a group you will find a heady feeling. Those who meditate will recognise it. You are in a state of Ether and if you use visualisation you can look back and see the Earth - much as the first astronauts did in 1969 .

Once you can do this, it's a short haul to showering that image with your group love. It may sound barmy, but try it first on your own garden/pot plant/ window box. (Have you tried it? *So - not so barmy, huh?*)

The Family Wish For Yule

Yule is a very family-orientated time. So, family wishes - for the recovery or help of a loved one, for example - are a good thing to do.

The family wish follows very closely the usual three-fold wish in a circle that is standard at Imbolc in many circles, and which was described in the chapter on Imbolc. (The first wish for the world, the second for a loved one, the third for yourself.)

At Yule, you can change this to be more personally orientated. And now that you can use your Tarot, use it here.

The first wish - for the world - could, for example, be for a *family* member either living in or from another part of the world; or who is involved with world affairs; or can influence them somehow - journalism, media, medicine overseas, for example. Take the World card from your pack and, as you make your wish, visualise that person, as strongly as you can, and the country in which they live, or the job they do.

The second wish - for a loved one - focuses on the King or Queen of Cups, obviously depending on the gender of the person in question.

The third wish - for yourself - should use as its focus the relevant Queen or King (Emotion/Job or Studies/Problems/Finance and Property (and no, I'm not going to conveniently remind you).

If in doubt - always use your High Priestess But remember that you must *never* use the High Priestess as a significator for *anyone* but yourself.

The card of the World is the last card we are going to look at in detail. It is the card of endings; completion. Satisfaction and moving onwards. The final cycle; new things follow. The World can auger many things - always positive. A levels, degree studies, ending of the divorce process (promising better things), new happiness after despair - but always querant led. In other words - he/she has brought about this new positive state of affairs, and should be congratulated. A new cycle in their destiny is about to begin, and they should revel in it - and so should you! Haven't *you* changed since beginning this book?

Across the dancefloor, he approaches. Remember not to trust him entirely - but your High Priestess is watching you, like the eternal chaperone. She smiles as he proffers his arm. Look back at her. She gives an imperceptible nod of her wise head.

Music!

Lights!

You're dancing with the Juggler!

Enjoy.

CCT, 1999.

Appendices

Shoeblocks, glitter, tutus, robes and drums.
All the paraphanalia you need to complete your dance routine

Index

1 - Tarot Street, or South/West/North/ Eastenders

Yes! Your very own soap opera! And where are we? In the pub, naturally! We shall call it The Full Moon, of course.

Let's look at the cards we've used so far. They have personalities, don't they? Also, they are numbered, so we know there are more 'episodes' to come. We're only at the beginning. We also know by now that the Tarot is cyclic, so that, just like the best soap opera, each plot can be recycled again and again, slightly differently, using the same characters. So it is with reading the Tarot. Each reading will need a different interpretation of key characters and storylines.

Okay. Who do we have so far?

The Fool

The innocent, the wide eyed ingenue that you just know is going to be seduced by Horny Harvey or Siren Cynth. Oh, aren't you rooting for The Fool as he/she makes one mistake after another; turning up at the pub when Horny Harvey is stroking the barmaid's thigh; believing Siren Cynth when she denies she's married with eight children. You love The Fool because you can see yourself there. The Fool is you, your children, your little brother or sister; your widowed mother who decides after a dream holiday to shack up with an ebony Adonis. Who is going to tell The Fool not to do it? What arrogant person is going to tell The Fool he's wrong?

What if he's right?

Soap operas use The Fool character a lot, not because their writers are Tarot trained (I'm sure some are), but because the audience identifies with them.. We all are very scared of making mistakes.

The Fool begins on a new journey in life, as all of us do, with trepidation. He does not know what is around the corner on his path. But he has to tread it.

The Juggler

Aha! Enter Jack the Lad, the streetwise one. The pub barman who knows when young Jimmy's had a few too many. The sixth-former, the prefect. The 40-something friend of your mum who really told you about sex - or even, brazen hussy, initiated you. The Juggler succeeds against all odds - which is why this book is titled as it is because with him as your dance partner you won't fail either. The Juggler is your first tutor - and he knows his subject well.

I don't have Welsh blood but I've loved the poetry of Dylan Thomas since my teens. Imagine Ffill Mitchell saying the following lines, and you have the essence of The Juggler.

> *'The force that through the green fuse drives the flower*
> *Drives my green age; that blasts the roots of trees*
> *Is my destroyer...'*

The High Priestess and The Heirophant

Ena Sharples, who I'm afraid I do just about remember, used to fold her arms and narrow her eyes when talking about the Tart with a Heart of *Coronation Street*. They were women poles apart.

The High Priestess and The Heirophant may or may not not be tarts, but they are as mystifying as Ena found Elsie Tanner, and I suspect that the actresses - Violet Carson and Pat Phoenix, both very spiritual women - knew they were guided by some other force when they created their roles; which became definitive performances of their time.

Probably, the High Priestess or Heirophant isn't a character in a soap opera so much as the ambiance, the feeling behind it.

The teacher whose insight gets the wayward Flossie through her A levels, despite her pregnancy and the fact that her father is a manic depressive transsexual fighting HIV and her mother's career in tightrope walking has been cut short owing to amputation of both legs following a helicopter crash which annihilated the village post office. The kindly vicar, the wise sage; the older brother who advises.

For the purposes of this lighthearted soap opera scenario - that will do for the High Priestess and Heirophant. But as you already know by now, they are far more important.

Most people I know do watch, or listen to, soaps. *Archers* addicts obviously have the edge on superiority - at least, they think they do - because it's Radio Four. In a way they do, for purposes of meditation and pathworking, because of course they must imagine what the characters look like. But all soaps have the soothing effect of the High Priestess and Heirophant - the calm, gentle touch on the brow; the whisper that for half an hour, or whatever, you need only switch off your conscious mind and fly with us, somewhere else.

That 'somewhere else' need not, of course, be somewhere good for you, but it does usually relax you. What you get out of the experience depends a lot on yourself, and what you want. Do

135

you simply want to be entertained, or made to think? Though some might dispute it, soap operas operate quite a lot on this dual level of choice.

So does the Tarot, and so does magic.

So, we've got The Fool sitting nursing a pint or a gin and tonic in The Full Moon and in comes his/her mum and dad, the Emperor and the Empress.

'Oh Gawd/oh dear' says Mum 'Your father's just won the lottery and I've been told I'm expecting again.' (Emperor with Ace pentacles and Empress with Ace Cups, Tower and Page Cups, perhaps! - and yes you will be able to understand this soon) . 'What shall we do, son/daughter, luv, go to Australia and buy Queensland or enrol the little one at Eton?'

Ah. But there are other people in the bar.

And the purpose of this chapter is to help you understand what are called 'the Court cards'. It is from the Kings and Queens that the significator is chosen, and so you need to know a little bit about their characters, in order to select one for you when you read for yourself, or to realise the huge hint you're being given when reading for someone else. They will choose a significator pertinent to their situation. They will. They do. And it will give you a clue.

The Queen of Cups

That attractive lady in pink - how sensitive she seems. How she knows her own vulnerability, yet she must be aware of the heart she wears on her sleeve. She picks up her glass carefully, like a golden cup, and she sips, her eyes darting around, conscious of any eyes on her.

Usually, she is here with her man and she feels anxious without him tonight.

Notice - as you are obviously in the bar with her - how the men are attracted to her and how they cast covert glances towards her.

And yet - you like her, too, don't you? If you catch her eye she will smile.

If you're feeling sad, you feel she will understand, don't you? Her eyes tell you this. You can talk to the Queen of Cups. You feel she would understand, emotionally.

(Diana, Princess of Wales, will now always be the archetypal Queen of Cups. She styled herself as the Queen of Hearts, which is the playing card equivalent to the Queen of Cups. She died tragically young, in love, and therefore forever beautiful. She will, whatever your views about the monarchy and Diana herself, become a British peoples' goddess in the future.

Because we are now a multi cultural nation, ethnic deities have limited attraction, perhaps, and the extraordinary effect on Britain of Diana's death is a classic example of the people searching for, and reclaiming, a Goddess figure - whatever your perception of her may have been during her life.)

The King of Cups

Is he gay? He seems so sensitive and understanding. Well, he might be, depending on who is sitting with him. If you see him with the Queen of Cups - no way. The King and Queen of Cups are the tightest lovers and the most steadfast. Occasionally Kings and Queens of Cups experience difficulties as we all do; but basically they are made for each other. They understand each other.

Is he on his own? Ah, well, then if you are an unattached lady, you could smile at him. Always smile at a King of Cups. Depending on your own status, he will become lover or friend.

Is he your friend anyway, possibly brother? Go and demand a drink and a packet of crisps. The King of Cups is always a lovely man. If he is your brother or your mate or your dad, introduce him to that shy lady in pink at the bar he's been looking at for the last five minutes.

In any reading, particularly if your querant has chosen the Queen of Cups as her significator (see 'Choice of Significator' in appendices) a King of Cups is important. He will represent a man whose presence in your querant's life is good for her emotionally.

In our pub, let us suppose the Queen is on a blind date. She's feeling emotional because this is the first time she's been out since her divorce. A well-meaning friend (probably a Queen of Wands) has organised this for her so that she can meet a man the friend knows would be perfect for her.

The King of Cups rises. Ah!... and approaches the Queen of Cups shyly. The beginning of a perfect partnership! The Queen of Wands was right. Infuriatingly, she usually is.

Kings and Queens of Cups : Always denotes a reading for the emotional aspect of your querent's life. The partnership obviously is to be encouraged. The only problem may sometimes be a lack of 'feet on the ground'. And sometimes a King of Cups may be brilliant emotionally but a bit useless when it comes to the practical things in life - like money. But not always. His other personae regarding his job, etc., may well be there too; as a King of Pentacles for example.

King and Queen of Wands

There they sit, and their body language tells you they get on well. The young couple who run the Italian restaurant together, maybe - or its chef and his lady boss. Perhaps the local head teacher and his deputy. They could be lovers but their main connection is with their careers, or studies.

In conversation he says, 'D'you know that stunner at the bar - that lady in pink?'

The Queen of Wands says 'Isn't that Isobel from accounts/reception/the kitchen/Ted Blogg's the boss's ex?'

The King of Wands watches ruefully now as the King of Cups joins his Queen. Too late, he realises, and begins thinking about the last lady he chatted up and how rude and prickly she was and - good heavens - how strange, she's just come into the bar!

Kings and Queens of Wands: Usually connected with work/studies/learning. With a Cup querant a Wand of the same sex is often a best friend.

Another scenario I play out with my students is that Mr King of Wands in this pub owns a shoeshop, and his wife, Mrs Wand, is a nursery schoolteacher. Here we get both the career and education aspects in. It also tells you that Mr Wand - although dedicated to his career, which satisfies him greatly, is not as ambitious for the money side of it than is the King (or Queen) of Pentacles. Bearing this is mind, we named Mr Wand's shoeshop 'Plodwells'.

The Queen and King of Swords

OOooooh! Isn't he sexy, thinks Ms Wand enthusiastically. And doesn't he know it! He has arrived on his Harley Davidson and is dressed from top to toe in black leather.

Ms Pentacle - who we have not yet met, of course, merely keeps a cool counsel.

The Queen and King of Swords are together tonight in the pub but it isn't always so, is it? However, when they are, what a fine couple they seem.

Their sexuality seems to ooze from them. Their confidence together gives them an arrogance which is attractive. But split them and - oh, dear.

The Queen of Swords will surround herself with roses, not for their beauty, and not for their scent - but for their thorns. She will not let you into her innermost secrets and how dare you try? Particularly if you are male and not a King of Swords. If you are a King of Cups, oh! Beware! You will get hurt, badly.

A King of Wands, being more philosophical, may fare better; a King of Pentacles will shrug her off eventually as life's experience but no man ever forgets a Queen of Swords.

The King of Swords is similar and his effect on a Queen - depending on suit - can be just as devastating. He will hurt them all, yes - even his match, the Queen of Swords. To a Queen of Swords he may seem the answer to all her problems, but he rarely is the answer to anyone's problems. Although - and this is the attraction of a King of Swords - finding out can be such fun - particularly physically! The King of Swords prides himself on his sexuality, and he is every (joyful!) inch masculine. I always advise a fling with the King of Swords, but he is never a long term prospect. Always attractive, quintessentially sensual, they are irresistable. So don't try to resist them. Just be aware that if you're the Queen of anything but Swords you mustn't marry them, and even that match is a daunting prospect. .

Kings of Swords in soaps are too numerous to list!

On their own, however, Kings and Queens of Swords very often denote sadness. A querant who chooses a Sword Royal as a significator is asking you for help and has a problem. . Arrogant he may be, but there's a reason why the King of Swords is the King of Swords. And the same for the Queen.

Kings and Queens of Swords : People who present, or the querent perceives them as problems.

Kings and Queens of Pentacles

Do you want the good life? Are you male and a workaholic? You're the King of Pentacles, but you know exactly where you wish to go with your career and you are good enough at it to attain your goals. The King of Pentacles is the owner of the Full Moon. Not just the Licensee - the owner.

That's him over there, talking expansively with those local businessmen/golf club members/freemasons. He is an excellent businessman himself, and as the putative landlord of this free house he knows that it's not his job to wear himself out behind the bar. He employs people for that, and networks with his customers. He is a bon viveur, since that is what is required here, and the King of Pentacles is always in total command of his business interests. He is the provider, the 21st century equivalent of the hunter/gatherer. He sees his role towards his family as one of total protection. He will have made sure they are all in a private medical insurance scheme.

A King of Pentacles will keep a lady waiting in the Full Moon until the phone call from the headhunter/Hollywood/the Goddess's PR Consultancy comes through.

The Queen of Cups can't hack him - she wants more emotional committment, and will wring her heart out sharing a man with his career. He can transform her - and very often does - from a Queen of Cups to her all-too-easy alter ego, the Queen of Swords, in six months.

The Queen of Wands might manage a reasonable affair but they would be very boring, discussing MS DOSs's and accountancy CD Roms way into the night. Great business partnership (ish) - but imagine the children! Would there be any? Well, yes, because lovemaking would happen in a very earnest and controlled way, for precisely that reason. (Shall we have a child? Yes. Very well then, this is what we must do until you conceive. Now go and remove that modem and put on this black lace bra.)

Seriously, the Queen of Wands with King of Pentacles is a very unlikely match. With such a relationship, you're looking at the boss poking the PA because the PA thinks it might be good for her career. There is, you see, no emotion at all implied here.

There is one classic case of a King of Pentacles and a Queen of Wands. President Bill Clinton and Monica Lewinsky.

The Queen of Pentacles is an equally astute lady. She needs the good things in life and isn't afraid to go out and grab them. If she's your boss (and in a reading she won't merely be your equal) she'll be fair but good at her job. Hard to be married to, unless you are a King of Pentacles, then - wow. Serious money, probably.

A King of Wands might survive, because he will be able to reason and leave her alone when she tantrums - which she will, because she's very clever, at the coal face, and tough. And a woman. The Tarot is sexist. We are not talking political correctness here at all.

Here at the Full Moon, she is of course the boss's wife, clanking with gold jewellery because he buys it for her to show how well the pub is doing. She would never be seen behind the bar, but smiles a lot at the customers as she sips Sauvignon in front of it.

Remember - we're talking soap opera here. A Queen of Pentacles in a reading is anything from the bossess in the launderette in which you work part time to the owner of the multinational company for which you work.

Queens and Kings of Pentacles - property, finance, security, ambition.

Now, before you order another drink from the barman/juggler, consider that now you're going to have to be clear-headed for a moment. We are going to be dealing now with the Knights and Pages, and they need major concentration.

Didn't you just want to know this? They can mean two separate things, and guess who has to decide what they are telling us? You do.

Let's consider them first in their not-so-popular modes. You've now met the parents, who are all in the pub. They have children! Ah!

Knights, when representing young people/offspring are generally youths. (Sorry! You can't even know their sex - but you can ask. A Tarot reader is exactly that. You are not a psychic.) Pages will be small children.

What you must determine first is whether a Knight or Page is there in the spread because he/she is representing the child of the querant, or whether it is doing it's other role in Tarot - in the case of the Knights, indicating movement, 'moving onwards', progress in the field indicated by that Knight's suit

- eg the Knight of Pentacles, progress in ambition or with property.

Pages, when not being small children, represent communication, discussions. The Page of Cups, for example, indicates discussions of an emotional nature, about love matters and things close to the querant's heart. The Page of Swords denotes minor quarrels - ie, communication of a 'swordy' nature.

Yes but how, you cry despairingly, do I know if the Page is a child of the querant or just a quarrel?

You just do. It's usually very obvious. If children are coming into to your querant's reading then the reading is to do with family matters. There will be an Empress or Emperor, indicating that that is what your querant is. Perhaps this is a break-up situation and the querant is concerned about one child particularly, which is why the Page figures. You may have the three of swords (heartache) with the Page in the middle. Ask yourself why. (Ask your High Priestess). You will get a feel. You will.

You've now met all the locals. On with the dance itself.

2 - The Choice of Significator

The Significator is the card which represents the querant. It is put to the left of the reading, and for the duration of the reading this card is the person having the reading.

You should choose a Significator even when reading for yourself.

Select a Court card (see 'An evening in the Pub') which has some significance to the reason you wish to give yourself a reading. The other thing that you can do - and only *you* - is to use your High Priestess as Significator.

Such a reading may well be quite powerful - but remember that it may not be suitable if you have a specific question. For example- Should I go for this job/promotion/course of studies? will be better suited to using the Queen/King of Wands. Should I marry Charlie? may be better with the Queen /King of Cups. But a general reading - What can you tell me about the direction my life is taking? is perfect for your High Priestess.

Never, ever be tempted to read for someone else using your High Priestess as *their* Significator. Your High Priestess is part of you. She will work for you, and you alone.

What about a Significator for other people?

Okay. You've visited the pub, the Full Moon, and you've a vague feeling about the Kings, the Queens, and their offspring. In any reading for someone else, it's vitally important that they select their own significator. You will offer them the four queens, or kings, depending on the gender of the querent; face up. Invite them to select one card to represent themself.

Tell them to select the card simply because they like it. (If you are attempting a reading for yourself, bear in mind the meanings behind the court cards and choose your Significator accordingly. *You know* that choosing the Queen of Cups will tend to lead the reading into the emotional field of your life.

You can choose the King of Pentacles if you're male and want to know where your financial/security/ambitions are going. If you're female and want the same - significate with the Queen of Pentacles. But only choose Pentacles if you are fiercely determined and ambitious. If you're part of team, a student, wanting to know about the future possibilities, you'll probably choose the Queen /King of Wands, or your querant will.)

A King or Queen of Swords choice will instantly tell you that your querant has problems, and this may be why he/she is consulting you. So bear that in mind. Likewise, if you are doing a reading for yourself and *you* have a problem, the King/Queen of Swords may be a good choice for you if the problem is really getting you down.

Obviously, if your love life is a mess you may be inclined to the King/Queen of Cups, but if it's making you really miserable, then the Court Swords may be the quickest route to some sound advice. Or, of course, in such a reading for yourself, you also have the option of the High Priestess.

As in all things regarding the Tarot - go with how you feel.

For example - I had a client on the very afternoon I'm writing this in the evening. She clearly had an emotional dilemma and she was a regular client; a woman who had, through

146

coming to me over the years, begun to recognise the cards and their meanings.

I asked her to select a significator but she queried this. She was worried that her knowledge of the queens (remember the pub?) would influence her choice. It would have done. So I simply turned the four queens face down, sloshed them around, and invited her to choose one of the four cards. It was the Queen of Cups.

At this point, and particularly with a known client, there's no point in beating about the bush. As a reader of Tarot, you are offering exactly that. Beware of people who claim they are 'psychic' Tarot readers. They may very well be, but at its roots that isn't what it's all about. You are a card reader. Your cards 'conjure' or stimulate the psychic abilities we all possess into action, and that's only possible if you study and devote yourself *to* that study, as with many spiritual doctrines. It's your beloved cards which trigger the left side of your brain when you read. You put yourself into the hands of Spirit whenever you connect yourself spiritually with your High Priestess. She is your link with the Divine.

She *is* you saying 'Spirit/Goddess/Universal Soul/Angels - help.'

As with all things eternal and mystical, if you ask humbly for help, you will get it. Rarely is it quite how you imagined it to be, however.

I like to ask my querants for a small personal item such as a ring, and place it on the Significator while the querant is shuffling. It's important that the item should have been theirs alone - not granny's heirloom, because granny's vibes might still be lurking. During the reading, you may find that holding the item in your left hand (if you are right handed, of course!) may help quite meaningfully, but experiment.When your querant has selected his/her Significator, name the card for the person, and if they have a nickname or use a short version - Pam, for example, or Maggie - then use that.

Simply touch the card, with the object sitting on it if you are using one, and mentally give the card your querant's name. Now put the Significator to your left on the table. Remember - always try to read in the same place. You will find that one place in your house 'feels' right. It usually faces east, although north is good too, but experiment if you aren't sure.

Your querant - or you - should now shuffle the cards.

3 - Finding the Cards

and a Salutary Tale

Throughout this book, the emphasis has been on your High Priestess. She is your inspiration, your focus, your muse - your Goddess.

She finds the cards. She works through your Tarot and with your own intuition which, through your tentative steps towards a ballet with the Juggler, you are developing.

To find the cards necessary for a reading you do this:

You 'call down' your High Priestess. Having begun, perhaps, by a quiet meditation or the ritual I always do - which is simply lighting a joss stick to the East and acknowledging Earth at North - bring the image of your High Priestess behind your eyes, at the point of your mind known as the third eye.

This is the image of your Tarot High Priestess - not, if you are pagan, your own visions of the Goddess. This is why, all that time ago when you were setting out on your own Tarot journey, you meditated so strongly with your High Priestess, and this is why it's vital that you can empathise with her image on your chosen deck.

When you have fixed her image clearly, you shuffle the cards. If you are giving someone else a reading, you pass the cards to them (after selection of the Significator) and they shuffle them.

It is important to shuffle well. Your cards will be cleansed before you begin (see 'Cleansing the cards') which means they will be in a certain order, which you - or your querant - must un-order.

When all these conditions are fulfilled, and you've been able to quietly be alone with your cards, shuffling them rhythmically and not thinking about anything specific (unless you want a specific reading, in which case, go for it) you will find that at some point you feel that you don't need to shuffle any more. Stop.

Now call down your High Priestess.

Ask her for a number. Deal off the cards until the number she has given to you is reached.

Let's suppose the number 7 flashed into your mind. (And a number will - always trust your High Priestess)

Begin by placing the first card on a 'reject pile'. When you get to the seventh card, place it face down next to the card your querant has selected as his/her Significator. (See 'Choosing a Significator') It's quite important in a reading that you keep the cards face down while you select them (actually, *they* select *you*, of course) because when you turn them over, their impact as a group is greater. One never reads Tarot cards in isolation!

Continue asking your High Priestess in this way for numbers, and build your reading.

I have been reading Tarot since 1969 and I hardly ever use a structured layout like the Celtic cross, although I do use it with students. My own way is simply to lay the cards out as they are given to me.

The High Priestess says 5. Count out to the fifth card and lay it. 16 comes. Count out to 16 and put it down. Just carry on until the end. You may have a double line of ten cards or more; you may have eleven, you could have twenty.

You may find that during your asking for numbers two came simultaneously. Put those two cards down together. You may find that you get an urge to select 14 - and a nagging 'voice' is saying 'and 15'. Use them both, together. Listen.

If your supply of cards looks like running out, place the unused cards on top of the other pile. Your High Priestess is very far from stupid and she'll advise you. *Trust.*

Trust your cards, and particularly, your High Priestess.

You may well find this is the hardest part of Tarot-learning to accept.

Now. Let's try to do a reading together. Suppose your initial batch of cards, for a *Queen of Cups* Significator, resulted in the following:

The Lovers. King of Swords. 2 Swords. King of Wands. Ace of Swords. 3 swords. 10 swords. The Fool. The Juggler. The World. 3 Cups. Ace Cups.

It might help you to actually put these cards out from your own deck, and then check the meanings for yourself, before you read my explanation. Put the Queen of Cups on the left hand side of the table, and place the others in turn, in a line from the Queen of Cups. If you run out of table space, just start another line.

Now. *Look* at them. Run your eyes along, from the beginning card (The Lovers) to the end. (Ace Cups) Is this a reading about her job?

No.

She has a lot of swords. So a rocky time ahead, perhaps?

And what should have jumped out at you right from the beginning?

Two kings, and one of them a King of Swords. Alarm bells!

Now, without saying a word, you have begun to build up a picture of this reading. You know it will tend to deal with her emotional life because she's selected the Queen of Cups. You are aware that she has problems to contend with in the near future and you suspect there may be two men in her life.

Okay. Now you're on your own for a bit. Refer to the meanings and look at your cards . Take a piece of paper and jot down the thoughts that come - just try to sort out a vague picture. This is just practice!

So, how did you do? One fault I find with my students is that at first they try to say too much. They look for answers, reasons, whys and wherefores. This first reading, before enhancement, is like the bare bones, upon which you will build as you enhance. All this reading is doing is giving you the general picture of your querant's reason for consulting you, or a flavour of her life. You aren't going to solve all her questions yet!

And this is why, when my clients come for readings, they are here for an hour. A Tarot reading lasting twenty minutes at a Psychic Fair may vaguely deal with your needs but a true reading will answer questions with all possible and *practical* solutions - not just vague waffle which could apply to any situation - one of the criticisms so often levelled at the Tarot.

Here, in front of you, is our mythical Queen of Cups' predicament.

The first card is The Lovers. This tells you that she has a choice to make, regarding her emotional life. Because she *is* the Queen of Cups this obviously has great significance, and because it's the *first* card, you can be pretty sure she knows of the choice and that's probably why she's consulting you.

You've already homed in on the fact that there are two Kings. Are they two aspects of the same man? No.

Why not? Because she has The Lovers - a Major Arcana card, following that of her own. It's obvious her choice is between two men. Also, having two Aces in the spread might tell you that this is a fairly new situation, or that the choice she has to make will bring about changes. You've seen the 10 Swords, the 'mini death card', so you know her life is changing completely. The Fool is also there, beginning a new journey about which she is unsure. She also has the World, so you can advise her that she has reached one of those cyclic patterns which form our lives. An ending and a new beginning.

This thought process, involving the important cards which should have 'jumped out' at you - if they didn't, I promise that if you work with your chosen deck and its High Priestess one day fairly soon they will start to do this - is not conveyed to the querant yet, but you've got the 'flavour' of the reading.

Now you can begin.

You start by mentioning the two Kings, because they are people, and therefore always the most important cards to enhance. You tell your querant that you want to find out more, and briefly explain the system of enhancing. (See 'Enhancing')

The 2 swords sitting between the Kings emphasises even more the choice between these two men - and your querant's dilemma over this.

You can then explain briefly the characteristics of the King of Swords and the King of Wands. You will ask her whether she can relate these to the two men in her life. Now - they may be lovers, but bear in mind other possibilities. She may have a loved relative - a brother, uncle - *not* usually her father since this would be represented by the Emperor - who is giving her grief, or cause for concern.

Your noting the two men will be likely to have meaning for her, if not; all the more reason for enhancing.

Let us suppose you've mentioned the two men, and their characteristics. In this theoretical case, our Queen of Cups has a dilemma (2 swords) in her choice (Lovers) between two lovers.

Questions

1. Which man is she currently with?

2. Is that relationship stable, or pleasing to her?

3. Where might she have met the second man in her life?

You should be able to work out the answers to these three questions by simply looking at the first four cards in the spread.

Cover up this next paragraph - don't cheat! - and take a while to look at your cards.

Answers

1. The King of Swords. He comes first, *before* the dilemma occurs.

2. No. The fact that he is the King of Swords to her Queen of Cups suggests that the relationship was rocky before the dilemma caused by the King of Wands.

3. Probably as a result of her occupation or studies.

So, let's continue. Have you looked up the meanings of the next three cards? Oh dear, yes.

In reading Tarot, it's important to be positive. Nobody comes to a Tarot reader wanting to be told of disasters, and that isn't what Tarot is about. It's *your* job to translate the cards into something useful the querant can take away with her/him.

So here is how you should explain this part of the reading.

Your querant already knows, because she does and because you've told her, that she has an emotional choice to make. It's work related. You have alluded to the fact, and she probably knows, that the chap she met in Accounts/the new Rep who arrived on Tuesday/ the bloke in the refectory is important to her.

You must now convey that the solution lies in her own hands. She has the weapon to deal with this aweful (in the proper sense of that word) choice she must make. (Ace Swords)

There will undoubtedly be heartache (3 swords) and a total change, a kind of death, or 'killing off' of one part of her life emotionally in order that rebirth can occur (10 swords).

But here, you can in all honesty leave your querant with a positive feeling. The Fool says that after this typically 'swordy' period she can look forward. She will be unsure at first, but like the Fool, she must turn the corner.

The Juggler following the Fool is often seen, and obviously a sign indicating the need for confidence in herself. The World counsels the ending of one cycle of destiny so that another may be opened up. Here, too, 3 cups will reassure her that she will have the support of dear friends or relatives. The Ace of Cups at the end of the spread enables you to say that emotionally, ultimately she will feel total fulfillment and joy in her new relationship.

This is just the beginning, though. Now you enhance. But before we go into that, a little more on reading in general.

There are bound to be times, in your early, tentative experiments with Tarot reading, when you think 'am I imagining this?' This actually, of course, is a question posed by all who wish to work with any sort of magic and have had some success. The answer is always no, you aren't, if the result has had some meaning for you. The High Priestess/ Goddess will always select for you cards which are relevant.

Here is a tale, which may also help novices who think they are alone.

I attend, as regularly as I can, weekend-long courses in magic and ritual held by a very respected witch of many years' standing. They are as much a celebration as a learning process and everyone is empowered by the energy created. At the end of 1998, I attended one which was on a general theme of *creating* ritual workings. 'My lot' here were demanding more than my twenty years' of solo witchcraft could give them in terms of ceremonial - a hedgewitch like me will work basically on instinct and intuition during the festivals, having cast the circle, because - of course - we are usually alone.

M, let's call her - surely not a surprise to some - had changed the format somewhat. For the Saturday night ritual (to which all previous hours of the weekend aspire and work) was not planned with M herself having some idea of its eventual concept - the subject matter was to be decided by the group at the beginning of the weekend. This time, we were to devise the purpose of the ritual for ourselves.

Rituals alone tend to 'happen'. You will cast your circle and work as you wish, celebrating or asking for help or simply, at the Full of the Moon, acknowledging and worshipping Her and that will be that. You will be in tune, hopefully , with the Lady, and your queries will be answered.

I needed guidance because I was becoming more 'high profile' in my area and I actually didn't know what to do about it, or even if I liked it and wanted it to develop. It wasn't, of course, up to me and what I wanted. I would get what was sorted out for me, and I would need to make of it what I could.

By the time I booked on this particular course with M I had been reading Tarot for 27 years, and professionally for 15 years. My own deck was 26 years old and I know every inch of every beloved bit of it. But it's a large deck, made from cardboard and painted then covered with stuff we used to call 'clear Fablon' - how amazingly old fashioned all that sounds now, with laminates and scanners and stuff. I can't remember exactly how long it took me to make the deck, but it was a labour of love. Well, it would have to be, wouldn't it?

I digress. Anyway......

For the first time on a M course I left my Tarot pack in its wooden box at home. - because it's heavy, and I wanted to take other things . 'Creating Ritual' was the title of the course and it seemed sufficiently specific. Nothing about Divination. Fine.

What happened was that the students were required to formulate the purpose of the ritual, and that purpose was, by eventual consensus, Divination. All forms of these arts were explored by the large group present, and in the end, a group of people including novices, initiates of long standing, the curious and the wise decided that the course ritual should be dedicated to the Tarot.

If you have jumped the gun, as it were, by flipping on to this bit, the 'how to' bit - quite acceptable in this book! - you may not yet have encountered The Tower.

I call it the 'oh, shit' card and I felt this sense of irony that magical night. The climax to the courses M holds is the Saturday night ritual and there was this one on the Tarot and what hadn't I brought for the first time since I'd been coming to M's courses? My cards.

But there was more. One of the 'initiates of long standing' had brought her Arthurian deck. So had another, providing us with two decks of the same dominion. The Arthurian Tarot bears as much relation to my own traditional/Greek mythology deck as a carrot resembles a washing machine. I had never even seen it.

The purpose of the ritual was twofold - to supply an answer to a personal question, which was to be privately asked, and to further supply the answer to a more global, general question. It was decided that this would be 'What does the future hold for the Western Mysteries?' (Western Mysteries = 'Wicca', or witchcraft as we practice it in the West.)

As is usual in a ritual work involving a number of people, roles are played. As well as the four quarters and Spirit, other roles are acted out according to the tradition of the ritual itself. I always like, and so does M, to leave the choice of actor for a particular role in the capable hands of - whoever. Spirit, the Inner, the Lady, the Gods - it matters not; but every single person participating will *know* in whom they trust this decision!

In this case, the Tarot had been decided upon and therefore the choices were of the Major Arcana cards themselves. So, they were shuffled by various people, and, once the circle had been cast, taken round the circle , face down, and offered to each present.

I drew the Moon.

And then I knew, because the Moon is intuition and guidance, that I was going to be required to read cards tonight, from a pack I'd never seen before, and whose illustrations were foreign to me, in front of a group of encouragingly like-minded people but still strangers as yet. There being less of us than the 22 Major Arcana, the pack was offered again, to four people, of which I was one. I drew the Lady of the Lake. Baffled, I turned to one of the owners of these cards, and asked her with what the Lady of the Lake corresponded in 'normal' Tarot.

And her reply was - 'Well, obviously, the High Priestess.'

Well. Obviously.

The ritual progressed and sure enough, the climax and the reading part was reached. M looked at me, and reader, boldly I went! Circling the table (round, of course - remember the legends we were using), the images of these Arthurian cards were superimposed by my own, and I knew exactly what each meant. There were three of us; the cards' owner, M and I, and I have to say it was one of the most amazing evenings of my life.

So *trust*.

Learn to trust, and love your High Priestess and she will never, ever fail you, even when you are confronted with cards whose images may be in an obscure Russian dialect.

Now, Blue Peter children - don't expect to try this at home next week. Don't think 'I've learned what Carolynn says this means, so I can go out and buy The Tarot of the One Legged Peruvian Eunuchs, and Rider Waite will somehow super-impose itself' - it won't. By 1998 I had been reading with my own deck for twenty-seven years. But it did happen and I tell it here to demonstrate the power of the cards if you truly want to work with them. It also shows how powerful the traditional images are.

4 - Spreads or not? The 'CCT' method.

From the previous notes you will have understood that my method of Tarot selection doesn't use 'spreads'. There are lots of books which will explain all sorts of different 'traditional', 'astrological', etc. etc. layouts. They do all have their place, but I find them restrictive.

Intuitive Tarot is exactly that. You are using your High Priestess and she is using your intuition. By all means use the Celtic Cross if you want answers to a specific question, or if you feel your question/ problem is more easily solved by a structured and definitive system of meanings.

I always use the 'unstructured' approach - my students call it, flatteringly, but probably for want of anything else - the CCT method. This is because the first rush of maybe eleven cards which are numbered for you by your High Priestess are all waiting to be 'enhanced' or made an awful lot clearer.

Remember that any reading must be looked at as a whole picture. By casting your eyes over the scene and taking a while to 'drink it in' you may get a certain feeling about the group of cards in front of you.

Relate that 'feeling' to your querant's Significator (see 'Choosing a Significator') and some cards may seem, in your instinctive reasoning, to stand out. You won't know why, but just accept that they will, and note them. Tell your querant about them. 'I feel this is important (name the card, and its significance or meaning) and this. And this.) They will always respond, and you aren't 'fishing' - a term I use when bad readers question their querants shamefully before they begin a reading, and is standard at 'Psychic Fairs' (or even - horror!

161

'Fayres'.) Avoid them. A reputable Tarot reader will work from a base and will not need to be peripatetic.

It usually runs thus:

Bad Reader (with lovely, confidence inspiring smile) :' So. Why are you consulting me? How can I help you?'

What Querant says: 'Well, I need help with my divorce which goes through next month and my youngest daughter is really stressed out by it so I want to know if she'll be okay and the other thing that's really worrying me is that my husband is being really awful about the money side of it and I'm worried I might lose the house. Also, my father is very ill and someone told me at another psychic fair that he would die by Christmas and it would be awful and someone else would have an accident on two wheels and my brother rides a motorbike. I went to a palm reader at another psychic fair and he told me there was a break in my life line at around 30 and I'm 29 now. I've lived in fear for seven years.'

This is written lightly and with humour, but the reality is terrifying. The paragraph above is a compilation made into a fictional happening, but all those things have been said to me over the years by my clients - *after* a reading.

The less you know about a querent, the better, in my experience. When you read for someone, you hold their life in your hands.

What we need is a psychic professional body. Russell Grant has started the process - he is President of BAPS, the British Astrological and Psychic Society, which demands a tested standard before one can become a consultant.

We need this in Tarot too.

5 - Enhancing

This is literally what it says it is. You can 'enhance' interesting or important cards with others so that their meaning becomes clearer, or questions can be asked.

I have never read about enhancing in any other books on the Tarot, yet I can't believe I'm the only reader to have discovered it. Am I divulging a long kept secret? I don't know, but I've been teaching my students intuitive enhancing for ten years so if I wasn't meant to no angry High Priestess has entered my dreams, yet.

Make the initial reading, which will probably be no more than eleven or so cards. (See 'Finding the Cards', and remember to ask. You may be given twelve cards, or nine, or two. *Your readings will differ from my 'norm'*)

Do your general reading of these - and it will be very general at this stage. Remember to look at the spread *as a whole.*

The time span of a 'CCT' spread goes from the first card after the querant, then, like reading a page of a book, ending with the last. The actual time span itself can be set by you, rather like you would set your computer or your alarm clock. That is in effect what you are doing, since no computer is as competent and capable of such amazing things as the human brain. While you shuffle, therefore, or your querant is doing so, imagine the circumstances of any queries you wish to be answered, and also imagine time. I know - it's impossible to imagine time, but you can always hold on to 'six months' or 'give me a year, please' . (It always helps to be polite). Remember, it is that image of your High Priestess behind your eyes that you are asking.

First - are there any people? (Kings or Queens) They should be enhanced. You may find that describing the personality of any Kings and Queens (back to the pub!) will cause your querant (or yourself) to exclaim 'That's my friend Sharon/ Auntie Bessie/ my boss - etc. The most common important figure is, of course, usually the querant's own partner and yes! beware! You have to sometimes intuitively know that the 'best friend' - mostly a cup/wands combination - is actually a lover, but in my experience gay people are receptive to your fumbling and they readily respond to your tentative 'there seems to be a very good female friend here' with the cheery reply, 'yes, I'm Lesbian.'

Isolate the cards to be enhanced. Usually, it's best to start by enhancing one at a time, beginning with those which were nearest the Significator.

Remember - try to see the picture as a whole.

That very first glimpse of the entire spread gives you a feel of everything.

Turn all the other cards you have selected for enhancement over, but keep them in front of you on the table. Let's assume this reading is for you.

You know what's going on in your life, so certain cards will jump out as being interesting, now you know their meanings. Some will seem of little significance.

Concentrate on the first card - or cards; you may well feel the first two cards should be enhanced together and *if you don't know ask your High Priestess who sits there waiting to help you.*

This is where your powers - or developing powers - of visualisation come in. There will be something on the card -

an image, a face - on which you immediately focus. With the Aces, for instance, I ask my querents to imagine themselves holding a heavy, exquisite gold chalice or an equally heavy, sharp sword. The Ace of Wands, the opportunity card, should be seen by the querent as a wooden wand offered by the unseen hand of another. The querent should visualise themselves taking it. Ace of Pentacles can be used very imaginatively because the querent's *goal* can be placed in the centre of the pentacle whether it be a particular house, job or book to be published!

When the querent - or you - can visualise this, ask them to look at their Significator and see themselves looking back as though in a mirror. Ask them to spread the rest of the cards face down in front of them and choose three cards from anywhere, and place them face down on their own significator. Do the same on all the other cards to be enhanced, bearing in mind that they should remember their visuliasations as they do so, *for each card in turn.*

If you are reading for someone else, now it's your turn, as reader. You, of course, won't know what your querent is visualising but you know what the cards mean so go with that, and your prime visualisation, your High Priestess. Select three cards for each card to match your querent's, and place them at the top, face down.

Now turn the whole lot over and read.

Each card from the original reading will be enhanced to give you a wiser, clearer picture of the options, the possible circumstances, and likely outcome.

Enhancement isn't easy, but it isn't that difficult either. Remember the keyword - trust.

You are an amazing instrument if you attune yourself. Your High Priestess is your exceptional violin.

What better accompaniment for dancing with the Juggler?

6 - Meanings of the Minor Arcana

These are what I call 'sound bite' meanings of the minor cards. They will infiltrate a reading, helping you to make more sense of the Majors. Their main use, in my own way of Tarot, is with enhancement. (See 'Enhancing').

The meanings below are indebted to Terry Donaldson, Principal of the London School of Tarot, and I have added my own bits based on my own experiences.

The meanings given here follow the traditional guidelines, but I have explained the suits at their beginnings because it is vital that their influence on your/the querent's life be understood.

A bit of revision

Your querent chooses the Queen of Cups as her significator. What is the reading likely to be about?

And if she has chosen the Queen of Pentacles?

Or the Queen of Swords?

You need to be able to *know* this, instinctively.

* denotes cards which should always be enhanced

Wan∂s

Career and studies. Correspond to the element of Fire, and the South quarter. Masculine.

Ace An offer, advantageous to the querant. Probably work or study related. * and the querant should visualise herself accepting the offered wand while she selects the cards.

Two Good advice given by the cards. An 'emphasising' card, although not so important in this capacity as the High Priestess. Can indicate travel. Look at the cards around it.

Three Keep your own counsel. Go with the way you feel to be right. Set an example. You can turn dreams into reality.

Four Working together. In a career-related reading, often indicates a small company or department where everyone is required to pull their weight to achieve a common goal. In an emotional reading, very often indicates the family unit.

Five A conflict. Be prepared! There could be competition, obstacles.

Six Victory! Easy to remember - the Roman numerals VI are the beginning of the word!

Seven Take things one at a time. A question perhaps of not seeing the wood for the trees. Sort each problem out individually, and then go on to the next.

Eight Things are speeding up! Can indicate sudden activity after a period of doldrums.

Nine Listen to colleagues and acquaintances. Can indicate a refusal to listen to good advice. Let people help you!

Ten Burdens and responsibilities.

Cups

Emotional issues. Corresponds to the element Water, and the West quarter. Feminine.

Ace New emotional attachments which bring happiness. Fulfilment.

Two A new relationship or a change for the better within an existing one.

Three Friends, loved ones, relations.

Four Friendship. Either the querant is making new friends, or someone is reaching out to her. Can indicate (with the two of cups especially) friendship which can turn to love

Five Where did it all go? The figure on the (traditional) card stares sadly down at three overturned wine goblets, the wine spilling out. What he forgets to do is to look around the corner - there are two other goblets there, presumably full!

Six Re-learning the emotional give and take. Often given to a querant who has been emotionally hurt and needs to gently learn how to trust again.

Seven Total emotional confusion

Eight The mystery card. Something is - quite literally - 'on the cards', which will change the querant's view of things. The querant would be advised to wait and see.

Nine Happiness! Celebration! Lovely card!

Ten Emotional commitment. Sometimes known as the handfasting card, after the pagan wedding ceremony.

Swords

Problems, conflicts - and how to deal with them. Corresponds to the element Air, and the East quarter. Masculine.

Ace A problem, but the sword is in your hand. You can deal with it.

Two Dilemma

Three Heartache. Can also indicate divorce, or leaving somewhere the querant has been happy - but be careful with this.

Four Respite. The lifting of depression. A nice sword!

Five The parting of the ways. Let it go. Futility.

Six Moving into a more positive frame of mind.

Seven The need to let something go. A kind of 'mini Hanged Man'. Your querant can't carry all those swords by himself!

Eight Frustration! Sometimes simply showing your querant this card and saying 'You feel like this' is enough!

Nine Loneliness. Feelings of isolation.

Ten The lowest point. A sort of 'mini Death'. From now on, at least things can only get better.

Pentacles

Material and financial matters; security and ambition. Corresponds to the element Earth, and the North quarter. Feminine.

Ace New financial opportunities. Can represent the querant's home. Very much a 'go for it' card.

Two Same job, different place. Can represent movement, travel.

Three Learning. New skills, new courses.

Four The 'having it all card'. And yes, your querant can! (An air stewardess who has been coming to me for six years gets this card every time. She has three lovers in three different countries and occasionally feels guilty about it. She visits me, the four of pentacles pops out, and she goes away perfectly happy.)

Five This card has two meanings. In an emotional reading I call it the 'nursing' card - the need for TLC. In a purely material reading it represents financial expenses which are not expected.

Six The generosity card - your querant's or someone's towards her.

Seven 'As you sow, so shall you reap'. Rewards for hard work and effort.

Eight Someone who is very good at what they do, and usually they know it. 'The craftsman at work'.

Nine Wanting and achieving recognition in the eyes of the world. A materially-minded person who likes the good things in life.

Ten Joint financial committment. Family security.

7 - Traditional, Very Brief, Meanings of the Major Arcana

(nb - I would advise always to enhance the Majors in a spread, but the ones starred must be enhanced)

0. The Fool *
A new and uncertain journey. Naivete. New cycle of destiny about which the querant is unsure.

1. The Juggler/Magician *
Go forward with confidence. Hermes, the messenger of the gods. New pathways. Go for it!

2. The High Priestess *
Your dancemistress. The reader's own spiritual card. Cannot be explained in a sentence! Read the book!

3. The Empress
The mother figure. Creativity, fecundity. The querant as mum, head of the domestic household, or his wife/mother of his children.

4. The Emperor
The father figure. Independence. The querant as father, head of the household, or her husband/father of her children.

5. The Heirophant *
The querant's own spiritual card. 'Send it upstairs'. Listen to your own spiritual god/dess, angel, guardian - whatever.

6. The Lovers
Emotional choice

7. The Chariot
Battles, fights. Be single-minded. You will win.

8. Fortitude/Strength
Inner strength given at a time of need.

9. The Hermit *
Time to re-assess your life. Literally - go into your own 'cave' and contemplate.

10. The Wheel of Fortune *
The Fate card. Go with your destiny.

11. Justice
The need for balance in your life.

12. The Hanged Man
A necessary sacrifice. Let it go.

13. Death *
Total, irreversible change.

14. Temperance
Cool it!

15. The Devil
Temptation. Also - are you just taking the easy way out?

16. The Tower *
Oh! Shit! An occurrence out of the blue which provokes that reaction.

17. The Star *
The wish card

18. The Moon
Intuition. Listen to it! The feminine side.

19. The Sun
Growth. Assertiveness. The masculine side.

20. Judgement
The 'getting better' card. Atonement.

21. The World *
Completion. The ending of a cycle of destiny so that a new one may begin.

8 - Cleansing your cards

You must cleanse your cards *after each reading for someone else*. At first, when the only person to use them is yourself, there is no real need but it does get you into good habits and it becomes second nature if you cleanse them each time they are used.

Cleansing is a ritual and therefore a dedication each time you perform it. As such, it will bond you to your cards and vice versa, which is what we are striving for. You can also address and purify your cards to the Goddess, and I give a ritual for this in this section, but it isn't necessary if you'd rather not.

Cleansing, however, *is* vital to remove your querant's vibrations from the cards and leave them ready for your next reading. It's remarkably simple, although time consuming, especially at first, but it must be done. (This is another reason I mistrust Psychic Fayres. There is no time to cleanse the cards before the next 'punter'. Oh, shudder, shudder!)

I teach my students to remember W C S P. Wands, Cups, Swords, Pentacles. The way I teach them to remember it is to imagine themselves standing over the lavatory (WC) sprinkling salt and pepper in from condiment sets. Very naff but it certainly makes them remember it.

Start with the Ace of Wands, and simply build the suit up, through to ten. Then place on top of that the King, Queen, Knight and Page. On top of that now goes the suit of Cups, in the same order. Then Wands, and lastly Swords. You now have your deck in a pile with all the suits in order. The top card will be the Page of Swords.

Now, on top of these, place your Major Arcana in order - From Fool, Juggler, High Priestess through to the World.

And that's it!

I keep my hand-made cards in a box which was specially made for them, and my Morgan-Greers, which are my enhancers - (you don't have to have two packs, I just do) secured with a rubber band in a square of green silk. The box which houses my main cards is wrapped in calico and then in black velvet. Whatever fabric comes into contact with your cards should be natural in origin, but its colour should be your own choice. Esoteric shops - especially the mail order ones - sell Tarot boxes and wraps. (See 'Sources')

A ritual for dedicating your cards to the Goddess

On your tray:
Your Tarot deck
a joss stick in a suitable holder
a red candle
cup or goblet of water or wine
a dish of salt
(yellow, blue, green and white candles in holders if you intend to cast the full circle, which isn't necessary but can be nice.)

Check in your diary or in a calender for the phase of the moon. Don't do this if the moon is waning (ie, after full moon). Wait until the new moon and use the ritual during the time between then and the next full moon - it's about two weeks so there's plenty of choice!

It doesn't really matter what time of day you do the ritual - evening is nice because it's more atmospheric, particularly if the moon is beautiful, but choose your own time.

It's not strictly necessary to cast a circle in order to dedicate items, but, obviously, if you'd like to, then go for it.

Pick up your pack of cards, and start with East. Light the joss stick. Pass the entire pack through the smoke of the joss and say your own words, on the lines of 'I dedicate these cards to the watchtowers/quarter of the East and Air, that they may give me guidance and intuition.' Visualise your High Priestess holding the Ace of Swords.

Move deosil to South. Light the red candle. Visualise your High Priestess holding a flaming wand aloft. Pass the pack through the candle flame (don't burn it!) and use your own words. South is Fire and governs confidence, assertiveness, courage.

Move deosil to West. Dip your fingers in the water or wine and run them across all four sides of your cards. Visualise your High Priestess holding a heavy golden cup on her lap, looking down into it. Say your dedication. West is love, emotion, healing.

Move deosil to North. Dip your (wet) fingers into the salt and pass them gently across your cards. Your dedication at North should be to the Lady and her consort the Lord, and you can either visualise your High Priestess holding a pentacle, or Earth herself. Your dedication should include a reference to our planet and the bounty of it.

This dedication can be used for all your ritual objects - chalice, wand, athame etc., and for magical jewellery.

9 - Breathing Technique

I use this to concentrate my mind on a reading while the querant is shuffling the cards.

Breathe gently and steadily in through the nose - count 1 2 3 4 5 6 7 8, hold 1 2 3 4 5, breathe out through the mouth 1 2 3 4 5 6 7 8.

Repeat for as long as you wish. Obviously once your querant has shuffled the cards, and given them back to you, you'll have to stop!

10 - Dowsing

Dowsing is a subject which obviously fills books by itself, but I do use it with the Tarot and Natural Magic, although I'm not, unfortunately, a born dowser. Unlike Tarot and Earth Magic, which can be learned by anyone, I really do think that dowsers are born, not made. But you can try.

Simply take a pendulum, or some dowsing rods. Now - I know that sounds like a Mrs Beeton's recipe for stuffed chicken (take a chicken and stuff it) - but -

The way to attempt dowsing is as follows:

You can make a pendulum out of almost anything. It's simply a weight on a string or chain which is allowed to twist and move freely. Pendulums are available at most New Age places now and by mail order (see 'Sources') . As with everything else, you don't have to have some wondrous crystal. The pebble that caught your eye in the wood, glued to a piece of natural string may work far better for you.

Dowsing rods can be made out of the sort of coathangers dry cleaners give away with your clothes, or they can be bought from 'Sources'.

The most important thing when dowsing is to establish your 'yes' and 'no'.

Simply hold your pendulum comfortably, usually between the thumb and first two fingers of your preferred hand; with the string/chain about 5 inches long.

Concentrate on stilling the pendulum. This is its 'neutral' position. Say to your pendulum 'This is my neutral.' Now think of a question to which there is a very definite 'yes' answer. This needs to be a really obvious one such as 'Am I a woman?' (Providing you are, of course) or 'Is my name (your name)?'

Wait. The pendulum will do something. My 'yes' is a clockwise circle, but yours may not be. Whatever the pendulum does - that is your 'yes'.

Now ask the pendulum 'Give me neutral.' It should gradually come to a stop and hang motionless in the neutral position.

Ask a question to which the answer is very definitely 'no'. For example, 'Am I the Queen of England?' or 'Have I got two heads?' Unless there is something very wrong with you or you are, indeed, Her Majesty; the pendulum will respond, and that will be your 'no'. My pendulum's 'no' response is to flick backwards and forwards diagonally, but remember - yours will be your own.

And that's it!

Remember that I think dowsers are born, however, not made. This doesn't mean you can't use dowsing, but some people will get a far stronger response than others.

A friend of mine whose child is allergic to some food additives takes her pendulum to the supermarket and dowses food. Another, into crystals in a big way, will dowse over a display of crystals for sale before she makes her choice.

You can also use dowsing to find lost objects - but again - the subject for another book and since my own dowsing is feeble - although it did work on finding my son's watch - it won't be my book!

11 - Sources

The following are organisations and mail order shops I can personally recommend, having used them myself. There are hundreds more, obviously, which are advertised in the many magazines available - and particularly in Pagan Dawn, the quarterly journal of the Pagan Federation.

Information: The Pagan Federation, BM Box 7097, London
                 WC1N 3XX, UK.
                 Information packs, advice, Pagan Dawn

Contacts: The Green Circle, PO Box 280, Maidstone,
                 Kent, ME16 0UL, UK
                 Newsletter

Mail Order   Sacred Moon, 27 Wyle Cop, Shrewsbury,
Catalogues   Shropshire,
                 SY1 1XB, UK
                 Everything from incense and Green Men to
                 statues of the goddess made to order. Very
                 comprehensive.

                 Pentagram, 11 Cheapside, Wakefield, WF1
                 2SD, UK.
                 Books, tarot, incense.

                 Sacred Earth, 6 Upper Orwell Street, Ipswich,
                 IP4 1HW, UK
                 Pagan wares with integrity

Adornment   Caduceus, 35 Carnarvon Road, Leyton,
                 London, E10 6DW, UK
                 The most beautiful pagan solid silver jewellery

FREE DETAILED CATALOGUE

Capall Bann is owned and run by people actively involved in many of the areas in which we publish. A detailed illustrated catalogue is available on request, SAE or International Postal Coupon appreciated. **Titles can be ordered direct from Capall Bann, post free in the UK** (cheque or PO with order) or from good bookshops and specialist outlets.

Do contact us for details on the latest releases at: **Capall Bann Publishing, Freshfields, Chieveley, Berks, RG20 8TF.** Titles include:

A Breath Behind Time, Terri Hector
Angels and Goddesses - Celtic Christianity & Paganism, M. Howard
Arthur - The Legend Unveiled, C Johnson & E Lung
Astrology The Inner Eye - A Guide in Everyday Language, E Smith
Auguries and Omens - The Magical Lore of Birds, Yvonne Aburrow
Asyniur - Womens Mysteries in the Northern Tradition, S McGrath
Beginnings - Geomancy, Builder's Rites & Electional Astrology in the
    European Tradition, Nigel Pennick
Between Earth and Sky, Julia Day
Book of the Veil , Peter Paddon
Caer Sidhe - Celtic Astrology and Astronomy, Vol 1, Michael Bayley
Caer Sidhe - Celtic Astrology and Astronomy, Vol 2 M Bayley
Call of the Horned Piper, Nigel Jackson
Cat's Company, Ann Walker
Celtic Faery Shamanism, Catrin James
Celtic Faery Shamanism - The Wisdom of the Otherworld, Catrin James
Celtic Lore & Druidic Ritual, Rhiannon Ryall
Celtic Sacrifice - Pre Christian Ritual & Religion, Marion Pearce
Celtic Saints and the Glastonbury Zodiac, Mary Caine
Circle and the Square, Jack Gale
Compleat Vampyre - The Vampyre Shaman, Nigel Jackson
Creating Form From the Mist - The Wisdom of Women in Celtic Myth and
    Culture, Lynne Sinclair-Wood
Crystal Clear - A Guide to Quartz Crystal, Jennifer Dent
Crystal Doorways, Simon & Sue Lilly
Crossing the Borderlines - Guising, Masking & Ritual Animal Disguise in the
    European Tradition, Nigel Pennick
Dragons of the West, Nigel Pennick
Earth Dance - A Year of Pagan Rituals, Jan Brodie
Earth Harmony - Places of Power, Holiness & Healing, Nigel Pennick
Earth Magic, Margaret McArthur

Eildon Tree (The) Romany Language & Lore, Michael Hoadley
Enchanted Forest - The Magical Lore of Trees, Yvonne Aburrow
Eternal Priestess, Sage Weston
Eternally Yours Faithfully, Roy Radford & Evelyn Gregory
Everything You Always Wanted To Know About Your Body, But So Far
    Nobody's Been Able To Tell You, Chris Thomas & D Baker
Face of the Deep - Healing Body & Soul, Penny Allen
Fairies in the Irish Tradition, Molly Gowen
Familiars - Animal Powers of Britain, Anna Franklin
Fool's First Steps, (The) Chris Thomas
Forest Paths - Tree Divination, Brian Harrison, Ill. S. Rouse
From Past to Future Life, Dr Roger Webber
Gardening For Wildlife Ron Wilson
God Year, The, Nigel Pennick & Helen Field
Goddess on the Cross, Dr George Young
Goddess Year, The, Nigel Pennick & Helen Field
Goddesses, Guardians & Groves, Jack Gale
Handbook For Pagan Healers, Liz Joan
Handbook of Fairies, Ronan Coghlan
Healing Book, The, Chris Thomas and Diane Baker
Healing Homes, Jennifer Dent
Healing Journeys, Paul Williamson
Healing Stones, Sue Philips
Herb Craft - Shamanic & Ritual Use of Herbs, Lavender & Franklin
Hidden Heritage - Exploring Ancient Essex, Terry Johnson
Hub of the Wheel, Skytoucher
In Search of Herne the Hunter, Eric Fitch
Inner Celtia, Alan Richardson & David Annwn
Inner Mysteries of the Goths, Nigel Pennick
Inner Space Workbook - Develop Thru Tarot, C Summers & J Vayne
Intuitive Journey, Ann Walker Isis - African Queen, Akkadia Ford
Journey Home, The, Chris Thomas
Kecks, Keddles & Kesh - Celtic Lang & The Cog Almanac, Bayley
Language of the Psycards, Berenice
Legend of Robin Hood, The, Richard Rutherford-Moore
Lid Off the Cauldron, Patricia Crowther
Light From the Shadows - Modern Traditional Witchcraft, Gwyn
Living Tarot, Ann Walker
Lore of the Sacred Horse, Marion Davies
Lost Lands & Sunken Cities (2nd ed.), Nigel Pennick
Magic of Herbs - A Complete Home Herbal, Rhiannon Ryall
Magical Guardians - Exploring the Spirit and Nature of Trees, Philip Heselton
Magical History of the Horse, Janet Farrar & Virginia Russell
Magical Lore of Animals, Yvonne Aburrow
Magical Lore of Cats, Marion Davies
Magical Lore of Herbs, Marion Davies

184

Magick Without Peers, Ariadne Rainbird & David Rankine
Masks of Misrule - Horned God & His Cult in Europe, Nigel Jackson
Medicine For The Coming Age, Lisa Sand MD
Medium Rare - Reminiscences of a Clairvoyant, Muriel Renard
Menopausal Woman on the Run, Jaki da Costa
Mind Massage - 60 Creative Visualisations, Marlene Maundrill
Mirrors of Magic - Evoking the Spirit of the Dewponds, P Heselton
Moon Mysteries, Jan Brodie
Mysteries of the Runes, Michael Howard
Mystic Life of Animals, Ann Walker
New Celtic Oracle The, Nigel Pennick & Nigel Jackson
Oracle of Geomancy, Nigel Pennick
Pagan Feasts - Seasonal Food for the 8 Festivals, Franklin & Phillips
Patchwork of Magic - Living in a Pagan World, Julia Day
Pathworking - A Practical Book of Guided Meditations, Pete Jennings
Personal Power, Anna Franklin
Pickingill Papers - The Origins of Gardnerian Wicca, Bill Liddell
Pillars of Tubal Cain, Nigel Jackson
Places of Pilgrimage and Healing, Adrian Cooper
Practical Divining, Richard Foord
Practical Meditation, Steve Hounsome
Practical Spirituality, Steve Hounsome
Psychic Self Defence - Real Solutions, Jan Brodie
Real Fairies, David Tame
Reality - How It Works & Why It Mostly Doesn't, Rik Dent
Romany Tapestry, Michael Houghton
Runic Astrology, Nigel Pennick
Sacred Animals, Gordon MacLellan
Sacred Celtic Animals, Marion Davies, Ill. Simon Rouse
Sacred Dorset - On the Path of the Dragon, Peter Knight
Sacred Grove - The Mysteries of the Forest, Yvonne Aburrow
Sacred Geometry, Nigel Pennick
Sacred Nature, Ancient Wisdom & Modern Meanings, A Cooper
Sacred Ring - Pagan Origins of British Folk Festivals, M. Howard
Season of Sorcery - On Becoming a Wisewoman, Poppy Palin
Seasonal Magic - Diary of a Village Witch, Paddy Slade
Secret Places of the Goddess, Philip Heselton
Secret Signs & Sigils, Nigel Pennick
Self Enlightenment, Mayan O'Brien
Spirits of the Air, Jaq D Hawkins
Spirits of the Earth, Jaq D Hawkins
Spirits of the Earth, Jaq D Hawkins
Stony Gaze, Investigating Celtic Heads John Billingsley
Stumbling Through the Undergrowth , Mark Kirwan-Heyhoe
Subterranean Kingdom, The, revised 2nd ed, Nigel Pennick
Symbols of Ancient Gods, Rhiannon Ryall

Talking to the Earth, Gordon MacLellan
Taming the Wolf - Full Moon Meditations, Steve Hounsome
Teachings of the Wisewomen, Rhiannon Ryall
The Other Kingdoms Speak, Helena Hawley
Tree: Essence of Healing, Simon & Sue Lilly
Tree: Essence, Spirit & Teacher, Simon & Sue Lilly
Understanding Chaos Magic, Jaq D Hawkins
Water Witches, Tony Steele
Way of the Magus, Michael Howard
Weaving a Web of Magic, Rhiannon Ryall
West Country Wicca, Rhiannon Ryall
Wildwitch - The Craft of the Natural Psychic, Poppy Palin
Wildwood King , Philip Kane
Witches of Oz, Matthew & Julia Philips
Wondrous Land - The Faery Faith of Ireland by Dr Kay Mullin
Working With the Merlin, Geoff Hughes

FREE detailed catalogue and FREE 'Inspiration' magazine

Contact: Capall Bann Publishing, Freshfields, Chieveley, Berks, RG20 8TF